# The 11-Step Guide to the 11+ Maze

## Aylia Fox

HANSIB

Published by Hansib Publications in 2012
London & Hertfordshire

Hansib Publications Limited
P.O. Box 226, Hertford, Hertfordshire, SG14 3WY, UK

Email: info@hansib-books.com
Website: www.hansib-books.com

A catalogue record for this book is
available from the British Library

ISBN: 978-1-906190-54-5

© Aylia Fox

Design and Printing by
Print Resources, Hertfordshire, UK

*For my beautiful daughter Sienna,
my inspiration...*

# Contents

_Erratum_

Page 25, line 22 reads: For the mixed, Chislehurst and Sidcup
beat Bexley.

It should read: For the mixed, Bexley beat Chislehurst and Sidcup.

3

# Foreword

**By Debbie Tompkins, headteacher of All Saints' Church of England Primary School, Blackheath, London.**

Secondary transfer can seem like a very stressful process as all parents aim to get their children into the school of their choice.  Parents can be confused by the different types of education that are available and the varied procedures for admissions.

This book will hopefully help to demystify the processes involved and guide you through them in an easy-to-understand chronological order.

As you read it, remember to focus on your child's strengths and interests. Find out about the pastoral care and support systems that the school has, as you will not know what assistance you may need as your child negotiates the complexities of  teenage life.

Other important factors to consider include the journey to and from school - will your child be able to cope with it as well as will they be able to participate fully in the extra curricular activities that will be offered by the school.

Finally, the best advice I can give is listen to your own instincts. Please don't take notice of playground gossip as comments can be based on perceptions rather than fact and everybody is different.

Focus on the right environment for your child - a place which will allow him or her to be happy, secure and to mature into a confident young adult who fulfils their potential.

# INTRODUCTION

## PRIMARY SCHOOL PARADISE

THE good news first! If you live in the south east London and you want your child to have an excellent education, there really is no problem at primary school level.

There are numerous state schools which Ofsted rate as 'outstanding' and many achieve way above the national academic average in government performance tables.

Some are, understandably, over-subscribed but many are not nor have short waiting lists. If you are flexible and willing to travel a couple of miles, the chances of your child being able to attend a really good primary school are high.

To illustrate this and focussing on the **London Boroughs of Greenwich and Lewisham** - as we will throughout this Guide - the following table shows the top 20 schools for Key Stage 2 results in 2011 (the percentage of pupils who achieved at least Level 4 in English and Maths)

- Brooklands – 100% (Greenwich)
- Rathfern – 100% (Lewisham)
- Grinling Gibbons – 100% (Lewisham)
- Cherry Orchard – 97% (Lewisham)
- Our Lady and St Philip Neri RC – 97% (Lewisham)
- Fairlawn – 96% (Lewisham)
- St Peter's RC – 96% (Greenwich)
- Good Shepherd RC – 96% (Lewisham)
- Brindishe Green – 96% (Lewisham)
- Christ Church 93% (Greenwich)
- Deansfield – 95% (Greenwich)

- Henwick Park – 95% (Greenwich)
- Halstow – 95% (Greenwich)
- Our Lady of Grace RC – 93% (Greenwich)
- Cardwell – 93% (Greenwich)
- Brindishe Lee – 93% (Lewisham)
- All Saints' – 92% (Lewisham)
- St Mary Magdalen 92% (Greenwich)
- Turnham – 90% (Lewisham)
- Baring – 89% (Lewisham)

* National average is 74%

There are also numerous independent primary schools within the London boroughs of Lewisham and Greenwich almost all of which achieve considerably higher-than-average marks in national tests.

So, in case you didn't realise it, you're spoilt for choice, which takes care of the first seven years of your child's school life.

But don't be complacent. The time goes quicker than you could ever imagine and by the time your child begins Year 5, if you haven't started thinking about secondary school transition, you'll probably be the only parent who hasn't.

However, there are parents who have been thinking about it since they gave birth and by the time Year 5 arrives they're completely obsessed, stressed and dangerous to know! Avoid them like the plague in the playground, they'll infect you with their mania and before you know it you will be just like them. Which secondary school is best and how to get into it will be your only topic of conversation at the school gates - not to mention at home where you'll bore your family silly and scare the living daylights out of the poor mite whose future you're trying to secure.

7

**Some obsessive parents plan their child's future from day one**

My advice is: be sensible, do your own thing and tailor your plans to suit your child's needs. Talk to people by all means, but don't buy into the whole secondary school transition fixation.

Choosing a secondary school IS one of the most important decisions you will make for your child, but choosing one does NOT mean he or she will get into it.

There are numerous factors for you to consider. More importantly, there are numerous factors which are completely out of your control.

And herein lies one of the fundamental problems...

Geographically, most people consider themselves fortunate to live in the boroughs of Greenwich or Lewisham. The SE3, SE10 and parts of the SE13 postcodes are some of the most sought after in London and go hand-in-hand with some of the highest council tax bills.

There's beautiful parks, historic buildings, links to royalty, a famous river and tea clipper, art galleries, coffee shops and an Olympic site all on the doorstep and it's just 20 minutes from central London on the train.

Put simply, the areas are affluent. If you live in, say, Blackheath Village or Greenwich itself, chances are you're middle class and not short of money. In the surrounding areas even if you haven't got money and you're not middle class, chances are you fake it or aspire to it.

All of which means you probably want what's best for your child and you're willing to dedicate yourself to achieving it. In short, you're a **pushy parent** and you're happy with that. And you should be. If pushy means determined to succeed then it's got to be a good thing. If it means at any cost and damaging others along the way, then clearly it's a bad thing. And, anyway, being a pushy parent helped get your offspring into the primary school of your choice and it wasn't even that hard, was it?

Bu it couldn't be more different at secondary school level...

**FACT: there are no academically outstanding state secondary schools in south east London.**

This statement is based on fact with regards academic achievement in the Government's performance tables. To put it into perspective, the 2011 national average for the percentage of pupils achieving 5-plus A-C grades at GCSE was 58.9%.

**In Greenwich and Lewisham only 36 per cent of secondary schools achieved higher than the national average.**

The highest percentage – **86%** - went to the convent school **St Ursula's** in Greenwich and the lowest percentage – **32%** - went to **Crown Woods School**, also in the borough of Greenwich.

Other higher achieving schools include St Thomas More RC school, in Greenwich, on 80% and Haberdasher's Aske's Hatcham college, in Lewisham on 78%. Other lower achieving schools include Kidbrooke School, in Greenwich, on 35% and Prendergast Ladywell Fields College, in Lewisham on 41%

This compares to the **Grammar schools** we will be looking at in this Guide where the average percentage is **100%**. (The lowest is 96%)

Currently, the most **over subscribed school in Greenwich is Thomas Tallis** with nearly four times the number of applications as there are places and in **Lewisham it's Haberdashers' Aske's Hatcham College** which has more than 11 applications for every place.

There are **12 secondary schools in Greenwich. Lewisham has 14. All of them are comprehensives.**

So in fairness there are some good and sought after schools in Greenwich and Lewisham, but they're all non-selective and the main factor determining whether you get a place or not is the distance from your home to the school gates. Also, whether you follow a particular religion, or not.

But for pushy parents good is not an option. Only excellent will do.

So, what do you do?

Well, if you've got enough money you may wish to consider a **private school** (also known as independent school) but be aware, almost all of them are selective, so your child still has to pass an exam to get in. And, if they stay there until the end of the sixth form your outlay is going to be well in excess of **£100,000** and that's just the fees.

So what most pushy parents do – regardless of their financial situation – is attempt to get their child into one of the excellent grammar schools in the neighbouring boroughs of **Bexley, Kent or Bromley.**

Or, if they haven't got the money to pay for a private school, they 'work' the system so that their child can go at a reduced (or in some cases 'nil') rate (more on this later)

And you can do it too. Fortunately both options have a lot in common in terms of the process which you have to go through to achieve your aim. Unfortunately there's a lot you need to know and many hurdles to cross.

But worry not, this straight talking Guide will tell you EVERYTHING - what to do, how to do it, when to do it and how to deal with what can be one of the most stressful times of your life.

Perhaps more importantly, it will reveal things that no other book or person will tell you because it's written from the heart by someone who has been there, got the tee-shirt and is now considered an expert. Full of anecdotes and down-to-earth advice, I guarantee if you take everything on board you'll be miles ahead of other parents - many of whom are clueless about the gruelling 11+ journey you are all about to begin.

According to a Chinese proverb, the journey of a 1000 miles starts with a single step...

Because you're reading this you've already taken YOUR first one, so only 11 more to go!

Good luck.

# PRE-11-STEPS

## <u>IS YOUR CHILD CAPABLE?</u>

GRAMMAR schools select pupils based on their academic ability. In order to get into one you have to pass an exam.

This is colloquially known as the 11+.

**And, to put it bluntly, unless your child is bright they've no hope of getting in and there's no point putting them in for the exams.**

Competition for places is fierce and I mean *really* fierce because there's far, far more applications than there are places (about 10-fold in some cases). There are also a lot of bright children out there and a lot of pushy parents who will stop at nothing to ensure little George or Georgina gets what they deserve.

For example, I know of a family who moved temporarily from Greenwich to Bexley and paid rent on a property during the application period. Because they were able to put a Bexley address on the application form it gave them a better chance of getting into the Bexley grammar school of their choice as distance from school to home was a factor for admission. Unfortunately for them, a rival parent worked out what they'd done and informed the council. The council investigated and concluded there had been foul play and the Bexley school offer they had hoped for was withdrawn. Luckily for them their child was extremely bright anyway and got into a better school in another borough. But this is what you might be up against. It's war and your enemy could be your child's best friend's mother.

So how do you know if your child is bright enough and capable of taking the 11+ exams?

Well, most parents just know. They know because, in most cases, it's obvious.

Proof, however, comes from school both in terms of test results and teacher assessment. Although there are no hard and fast rules, **if your child is achieving Level 4b or above in English, maths and science at the beginning of Year 5, you can be pretty sure they're bright.**

**Key Stage 1 SATS results are an in indicator too.**
I emphasis indicator though. At this young age children's attainment levels do not necessarily reflect their attainment levels in Years 5 and 6.

Is your child the clever type?

**However, if they are at Level 2c or 3a then they're considered bright.**

On a more basic level, if your child is in the top set for English and maths and they go to a fairly high achieving primary school, chances are they're pretty bright.

And if they're bright and they've got a high reading and spelling age, they are likely to cope with the 11+ better than a child with average or below average attainment in these areas.

So, once you've established they're able, you should consider what you're letting them in for if you decide to put them in for the 11+. Bear in mind if you want to increase their chances of getting into a grammar school, they'll have to do two or three different education authority's exams. Each authority sets more than one paper, which means they could easily end up doing eight separate exams – more if they do independent schools ones too.

Is your child up to this, will your child be able to handle the pressure and will your child be prepared to put in the hard work before hand? The exams are NOT easy and even bright, high achieving children have to do a lot of preparation and revision.

Perhaps as importantly, are **YOU** prepared to commit to the process which, if done properly, can take up more than two years of your life? One thing you can be sure of is that it won't be an easy ride. Your child may well want to go to a grammar school but it's unlikely they'll be sufficiently driven to do what it takes. *You'll* have to be driven for them which do not sit comfortably when all they want to do is slump in front of the TV/DS/X-Box/laptop when they come in from school and all you want them to do is ANOTHER practice paper.

There'll be tears, tantrums, rows and retributions. There will be times when you think it would be easier to settle for the local comprehensive. But don't, you will regret it. If your child's bright, they deserve to be given the opportunity, so decide to enter them into the exams and then draw up a plan of action.

# STEP 1

## IDENTIFY SCHOOLS AND DECIDE WHICH YOU'RE INTERESTED IN

There are **164** grammar schools in England, **39** of which are in three neighbouring areas to south east London – that's nearly one quarter. We are, therefore, very lucky to have so many excellent schools nearby. However, as one of the areas – Kent – is geographically enormous, it is realistic to state that there are **10** grammar schools in three local authority areas within relatively easy reach of south east London.

They are:

## LONDON BOROUGH OF BEXLEY

### Chislehurst and Sidcup Grammar School (mixed)

*Hurst Road, Sidcup, Kent DA15 9AG    tel: 020 8302 6511
website: www.csgrammar.com*

*Headteacher -  Nigel Walker*

### Bexley Grammar School (mixed)

*Danson Lane, Welling, Kent DA16 2BL   tel: 020 8304 8538
website: www.bexleygs.co.uk*

*Headteacher – John Welsh*

**Townley Grammar School (all-girls)**

*Townley Road, Bexleyheath, kent DA6 7AB   tel: 020 8304 8311*
*website: www.townleygrammar.org.uk*

*Headteacher – Desmond Deehan*


**Beths Grammar School (all-boys)**

*Hartford Road, Bexley, Kent DA5 1NE     tel: 01322 556538*
*website: www.beths.bexley.sch.uk*

*Headteacher – James Skinner*

- *Do not be confused because each of the Bexley schools has a Kent postal address. The schools **are** run by the London borough of Bexley.*


# KENT COUNTY COUNCIL

**Dartford Grammar School for Girls (all-girls)**

*Shepherd's Lane, Dartford DA1 2NT     tel: 01322 223123*
*website: www.dartfordgrammargirls.kent.sch.uk*

*Headteacher – Sharon Pritchard*


**Dartford Grammar School (all-boys)**

*West Hill, Dartford, DA1 2HW   tel: 01322 223039*
*website: www.dartfordgrammar.kent.sch.uk*

*Headteacher – John Oakes*

**Wilmington Grammar School for Girls (all-girls)**

*Wilmington Grange, Parsons Lane, Wilmington DA2 7BB*
*tel: 01322 226351*
*website: www.wgsg.co.uk*

*Headteacher – Maggie Bolton*

**Wilmington Grammar School for boys (all-boys)**

*Common Lane, Wilmington, Kent DA2 7DA   tel: 01322 223090*
*website: www.wilmingtongrammarboys.kent.sch.uk*

*Headteacher – Andrew Williamson*

# THE LONDON BOROUGH OF BROMLEY

**Newstead Wood School (all-girls)**

*Avebury Road, Orpington BR6 9SA   tel: 01689 853626*
*website: www.newsteadwood.bromley.sch.uk*

*Headteacher – Elizabeth Allen*

**St Olave's School (all-boys)**

*Goldington Lane, Orpington BR6 9SH   tel: 01689 820101*
*website: www.saintolaves.net*

*Headteacher: Aydin Onac*

*All headteachers' names correct at time of going to press.

**Each of these schools has an excellent academic record. At Key Stage 4 in 2011 all of them - apart from Wilmington Boys and Girls and Chislehurst and Sidcup - achieved 100% success in terms of pupils achieving 5-plus GCSEs at A-C grade.** (Wilmington Boys got 96%, Wilmington Girls got 98% and Chislehurst and Sidcup got 99%.) The national average was 58.9%.

There are, however, numerous factors for consideration with regards which schools you may or may not be interested in.

Here are the things you may wish to consider:

- **Single-sex or mixed?**
  Some research shows that girls achieve better academically in a single-sex school, while boys achieve better in a mixed school. But even the most pushy parent must surely admit that the school experience has more than just an academic aspect to it, not least of all the chance to learn life skills. Your view on what's best for your child is likely to be coloured by what type of school you went to. Try to ignore this though, because it's highly unlikely your education will be anything like your son or daughter's – whatever school they go to. It's more sensible to think about your child's personality and their ability to interact. Most girls of 10 and 11 despise boys, but seem able to deal with them. Boys, meanwhile, tend to develop an interest in girls that bit earlier, although their social skills tend not to develop until much later. Do you think a boy would distract your girl? Is there any evidence of this so far? Do you think your boy would be

distracted by girls? What's the evidence so far? And, why not ask your son or daughter what they would prefer. Maybe their answer will help as you agonise over what is generally thought of as one of the more tricky decisions with regards secondary transition.

**And, to help you decide, here are the two opposing views presented by two well known London headteachers**

*Lisa Laws, Headteacher of Blackheath High School for Girls in Blackheath, believes single-sex education is best. She says:*

"There is much evidence that girls perform better and achieve more widely in single-sex schools and this is reflected in the disproportionate share of top league table positions taken up by girls' schools.   A study of value added between 2002 Key Stage 3 and 2004 GCSE results in England, suggests that pupils do, in fact, record greater progress in single-sex schools (Malacova, 2007).

Academic studies and educational experience tend to show that girls and boys have different learning styles and preferences, as well as needs, which are best addressed on their own terms.  They also tend to mature at different rates.  In single sex schools, these things can be fully accommodated, without any conflict of interest.  The Girls' Day School Trust states that "Research has shown that merely separating girls from boys has little impact in itself – beneficial results flow only if this goes in lock-step with a self-conscious and sustained attention to girls' learning preferences, needs and styles; through attention to, among other things, curriculum opportunities and expectations, teaching strategies and physical environment – in short, the whole-school culture."

When they are given their own dedicated space in which to develop, girls achieve more. There is much evidence to support the fact that, in single-sex schools, girls:

- perform better in examinations
- are less constrained in their choice of subjects
- have more opportunities to show leadership and
- are more successful in the job market.

Single-sex schools ensure an environment that is free of gender-stereotyping, distraction and harassment; together with a refusal to allow people to typecast themselves according to others' perceptions. This is reflected in the wide-ranging subject choices offered by single-sex schools. E.g. at Blackheath High School, Mathematics, the Sciences and Languages are amongst the most popular choices at A level.

It is a fact that girls achieve better educationally than boys at the age of sixteen, and a higher proportion of girls continue in education to degree level. In addition, a longitudinal study, undertaken by the Institute of Education, found that girls who attended all-girls' schools went on to earn higher wages than girls from mixed schools (Sullivan, 2006).

The outcome of an outstanding education should leave young people with more than just GCSE and A level certificates. It should help them to develop the qualities, competencies and skills that will help them to make a success of their adult lives. Education should widen horizons and give young people choices. I compare qualifications

21

with keys to doors; the better the qualifications, the more keys a young person acquires to those doors. However further progress will depend on personal qualities such as their social skills, work ethic, sense of responsibility, leadership skills, initiative & resilience.

All of these qualities, I believe, are most effectively developed in a single-sex environment where young people are empowered to achieve everything they are capable of – and more."

*__Richard Russell, Headteacher of Colfe's School in Lee believes co-education is best. He says:__* "The most compelling argument for coeducation is also the most obvious: the increasing numbers of parents who choose coeducation and reject single-sex do so because they want their children to grow up in an environment which prepares them for a world which contains both men and women. They do not want their daughters to be finding out for the first time in the induction period at Ernst and Young that little boys (of whatever age) can be very silly. Boys, on the other hand, should not be leaving it too late to discover that girls tend not to do Warhammer and Arsenal.

But the benefits of coeducation extend beyond the obvious aspects of preparing for life in general. The educational experience itself is enriched by the presence of both male and female perspectives in classrooms and laboratories. Discussion of literature, to take just one example, is immeasurably richer in the coeducational classroom. The social balance of the coeducational school enables boys and girls to learn from each other in a wider sense, breaking down the intensity of difficult social dynamics which can so easily develop when boys or girls are left to their own devices.

Coeducation excels outside the classroom as well. Coeducational schools are free to extend the theatrical repertoire beyond *Twelve Angry Men* and *Daisy Pulls it Off*. The awful alternative (boys in drag) becomes equally a thing of the past. On the sports field, girls play football and cricket, as rounders and lacrosse lose their kudos.

In their anxiety not to become a complete anachronism, advocates of single-sex schools point with growing and boring insistence to the fact that they continue to dominate the higher reaches of the league tables. It is frequently claimed that girls in particular get better results in single sex schools. But the most authoritative recent research suggests otherwise. It was commissioned by the Headmasters' and Headmistresses' Conference which represents the heads of 250 leading independent schools in the UK. The research covered schools in Australia, New Zealand, Canada, Ireland and the USA, as well as Great Britain and Ireland. *The paradox of single-sex and coeducational schooling* http://wordpress.buckingham.ac.uk/wp-content/uploads/2010/10/hmcsscd.pdf concludes that boys and girls in single-sex schools enjoy no perceptible academic advantage and the author of the report, Sir Alan Smithers, is the foremost educational adviser in the UK.

Sir Alan's conclusion could not be clearer: "While both single-sex and coeducation have passionate advocates, half a century of research has so far revealed no striking differences one way or the other."

23

It should also be noted that an increasing number of boys' schools are now admitting girls, making them coeducational, whereas very few girls' schools choose to open their doors to boys (save for the sixth form). Could this be a sign of increasing desperation on the part of antiquated female heads to support the bogus claim that single sex education for girls is, ipso facto, superior to the co-educational alternative?

I firmly believe that the choice between single-sex and co-ed is not about results but about ethos and a belief in how you best prepare children for adulthood. My own school, Colfe's, has been fully co-educational for more than a decade. We are comfortable with our ethos, but not complacent: a standing coeducation committee meets regularly to discuss gender issues and will continue to do so for the foreseeable future. Meanwhile our pupils will continue to benefit from both male and female perspectives in all aspects of school life."

## Distance from home

Starting secondary school normally means the beginning of daily independent travel for your child. This is a big step for them and you need to be sure they can handle whatever journey a particular school dictates. Most secondary schools are not on people's doorstep so your child is no different from any other in that they will have to become accustomed to getting up a lot earlier than they did at primary school. But no parent should expect their child to spend hours commuting every day – even if it means they can attend the best school on the planet. You have got to be sensible. If the school journey means they've no time to do their homework, let alone extra curricular activities or meeting up with friends, then it's clearly inappropriate. And, many people consider that if it takes more than an hour each way and involves more than two modes of transport, it's too long. Do some research on the various different ways of getting to a school and do a practice run with your child. That way you know exactly how your child will be feeling twice a day, five days a week for the next seven years.

## Academic achievement

While all the above grammar schools achieve academically well, there is still competition between them and a hierarchy. Two of the schools are known as super-selectives because they only take the most able children (based on the entrance exam) and they out-perform the others by a mile. They are Newstead Wood and St Olave's. In the Sunday Times' 'Top 100 State Secondary Schools' published in November 2011, St Olave's was rated number 5 and Newstead number 17. None of the other grammars came in the top 100.

**In 2011's GCSE results the pecking order of the girls' grammars was: Newstead Wood, Townley, Dartford then Wilmington. For the boys it was: St Olave's, Dartford, Beths and Wilmington. For the mixed,** ~~beat~~ Bexley **Chislehurst and Sidcup** ~~beat Bexley.~~

( see Erratum on page 3 )

## Specialist status

All the grammars have been awarded specialist status in a particular subject or group of subjects. My advice is to take almost no notice of it. It really won't affect your child on a day-to-day basis. So, do not fret if you have set your heart on, say, Beths, but your son is not a whizz at technology or languages (the school's specialisms). The benefit to the school of having specialist status is that it attracts extra funding for those subjects. Also, the specialisms tend to be ones like maths, computing, languages, technology, science and sport. There are no creative or literary ones like English or psychology.

## Size of school

All secondary schools are much bigger than primary schools, but some are bigger than others. The advantage of a big school is that their Year 7 intake is likely to be bigger than a smaller school's, and they may well have better facilities and a wider choice of subjects on offer. For example, Chislehurst and Sidcup has 1334 pupils on its roll and a Year 7 intake of 192. This compares to a smaller school such Wilmington Grammar School for Girls which has 810 pupils and a Year 7 intake of 120. And Dartford Grammar School for Girls has 1120 pupils on its roll and a new state of the art leisure centre and swimming pool while Wilmington Grammar School for Boys has 900 pupils on its roll, limited leisure facilities and no swimming pool...

## Extra Curricular Activities

At school open days one of the most frequently questions asked by parents is what sort of clubs and activities does the school have? I personally think it's a pretty pointless question because all the grammar schools have an endless list of clubs and activities. There really is something for everyone and I suggest it's not one of the more important of issues when choosing a secondary school. Having said that, some schools have a reputation for a particular extra-curricular activity. For example, Chislehurst and Sidcup School is historically linked to sport and, in particular rugby; while Townley is favoured by artistic and creative types due to its interest in performing arts. So, it's worth thinking about what the school excels in with regards to non-academic things, but to my mind it shouldn't be a deal breaker. If the school meets your requirements in everything else, just go for it.

**Cohort Spectrum**

It's a good idea to consider where your child would stand in their class and/or year group in terms of a range of abilities such as academic achievement, sports, sociability, confidence, popularity etc. So in one school – for example Bexley Grammar – they might be an academic star and top of their class, while in Newstead or St Olave's they could easily be the struggling lowest achiever. Such situations can have a positive or negative affect on a child's self-esteem and, as such, should be a matter of some concern.

**What Your Child Wants**

It's quite likely that before you ask your child what school they might like to go to, that they've already decided. Their decision, however, is likely to be based on playground gossip, not to mention the colour of the uniform and what sort of food they serve at lunchtime. Peer pressure is a big issue in Year 6, particularly if your child's friends have pushy parents. Everyone knows which the good schools are and which are the really good schools and children often aspire to get into the school their friends are talking about.

So listen to what they say and their reasons for saying it, but remember YOU are undoubtedly a better judge of what's best for them. Problems arise when you have to decide how far to push to convince them that your choice is the right one. My advice is to take a common-sense approach. Communication and negotiation are vital, but you have the power of veto and the child must accept and respect that. But don't lose sight of the fact that it's your child – not you – who will be attending the school and it's therefore crucial that you provide them with a sense of ownership in the decision – even if they don't have the casting vote.

## Siblings

Does your child have a brother and sister at a grammar school already? If so, it can be very useful in terms of getting your next one in too. Some of the schools have a sibling policy in their over-subscription criteria. In Wilmington Boys and Girls Grammar School and Dartford Grammar School for Girls it is the second most important factor if the school is oversubscribed. At Beths it is third and at Bexley it's fourth. This also means that these schools might be more difficult to get into because many parents want one child to go to the same school as the other. You might feel the same. It certainly helps from an organisational point of view and most parents would agree that it's psychologically good for siblings to know they've always got a 'friend' in the building. On the downside, you need to remember that your children are individuals and just because one school suits one of them, does not mean it will be suitable for another. Some children will fare better out of the shadow of their sibling, some might suffer and some won't care. It's worth at least asking each one what they think and then make an informed decision.


**Academy or Not?**

Academies are publicly-funded state schools that have independence in their governance.

They are not controlled by the local authority; they set their own pay and conditions for staff; they can choose how they deliver the curriculum and they can change things like the length of terms and school days.

They have been the subject of political controversy because the last Labour Government initially set *some* up to replace under-performing schools and ruled they had to have a sponsor. That sponsor could be a business, a successful school, a university, a charity or a faith body, amongst others. Sponsors were – and still are - held accountable for improving the performance of the school and had – and still have - the freedom to do this by changing traditional and established aspects of education.

Supporters view academies as visionary and claim the private investment helps tailor education to meet pupils' particular needs. Critics believe that sponsors such as businesses could influence educational policy in a self-serving way and that educational 'privatisation' is socially divisive.

Academies receive their funding from the Department of Education, rather than the local authority, although the amount remains the same per-pupil. Academies do, however, have greater freedom over how they spend their budgets to best benefit their students and it is this aspect that particularly attracts those who run schools.

Increasingly, schools (of all sorts) want to become an academy. In May 2010 there were 200 in England and Wales. In March 2011 there were 1,529.

**Of the 10 grammar schools in Bexley, Kent and Bromley, 8 are now academies. The only two yet to convert are Townley Grammar School for Girls and St Olave's.**

Ask any head of any of the other eight grammars what difference being an academy makes to a pupil on a day to day basis and they will probably say "nothing." This is undoubtedly true. The schools don't change their name, impose a new uniform or do anything outrageous like abolish the school prom; they just carry on as usual. It's mainly admin and behind the scenes things that changes.

Once you've considered all of the above points you should draw-up a long, short-list based on the factors that are important to you. So, for example, if you know you want a mixed school, then the only ones on your long short-list will be Bexley and Chislehurst and Sidcup. If you know that you do not want your child to travel more than 'x' amount of miles and three of the schools are further away than that, then you can immediately discount them.

What a lot of people do, however, is keep their options open at this stage and draw up a long short-list of all the schools that their child would be eligible to attend if the pass the tests (obviously a boy cannot go to a girls' school and vice-versa!) This, in my opinion, is the sensible way to proceed.

# STEP 2

## RESEARCH

"If we knew what we were doing, it would not be called research would it?" Albert Einstein

Research comes in 4 main forms:

1) **Documentation** about the school in the form of prospectuses, Ofsted Reports, the school's own website, profile, annual report and online educational forums

2) Education authorities' **brochures**

3) Visits to the school in the form of **open day**s and evenings.

4) **Talking** to people who have a child at the school or people who know more about it than you.

The earlier you start research, the better in my opinion. But keep it in perspective. There really is no need to start attending open days if your child is in Year 3. Year 4 – yes, it's a good idea to see with your own eyes what you've been reading about in order to form preliminary opinions. But, be sensible and remember that what might be suitable for your child when they're 8, could be vastly different to what's best for them when they're 11.

## Documentation

Read, read and read a little more.

Without losing yourself under piles of paper, digest as much information as you can find. Ring up the school and ask them to send you their up to date prospectus. Log-on to Ofsted's website and obtain their latest report on the school. Some will be more than three years old, but don't let that worry you. Good grammar schools don't fundamentally change in a couple of years, although there might be educational infrastructure changes such as the common occurrence nowadays of a school becoming an academy (more on that later). The school's website will be a treasure chest of information and, remember, you can print it out. Just be aware as you're reading it that it will all be positive. No organisation draws attention to its weaknesses and schools are no different. Do your best to read between the lines and compare school websites. If a website is out-of-date and littered with spelling mistakes then it probably tells you something about the school in general and, specifically, about its attitude to literacy. The internet is packed with educational websites and forums. Many are devoted to 11-plus issues. See the back of this book for a selection of them.

Read as much as you can but don't get lost under a mountain of paper

## Education Authority Brochures

All education authorities are legally obliged to produce some sort of publication that gives the information you need in order to apply for a school within their jurisdiction. They are published every 12 months in order to take into account of changes from the previous year and are normally available in the summer before the following year's intake (i.e for September 2012 admissions, the brochures came out between June and September 2011) They all have similar names. Bexley's is: 'Admission to Secondary Schools in Bexley'. Kent's is: 'Admission to Secondary School in Kent' and Bromley's is: 'Moving on to Secondary School in Bromley'. There are three ways to obtain them – 1) Call the education department of the authority and request one is sent out to you in the post (be warned, though, Bromley doesn't like doing this and refers you to its website. Best thing to do is say you need it urgently and haven't got access to a computer) 2) Obtain them via the authority's website and print them out (be warned though, this can take up 60-pages of A4) and 3) Visit a library in the borough and hope they have some in stock. This also applies to the HQ of the authority concerned (not very realistic to trail to and from Maidstone, however, where Kent County Council is based).

These brochures are essential because they give you lots of specific information about all the (state) schools in the borough - both selective and non-selective. So, for example, you can go to the page where the school you're interested in is listed and find out things like how many pupils they can admit in Year 7; how many pupils attend the school; the admissions contact; the school's specialism's; the oversubscription criteria (more on that later) and when the

33

open days/evenings are. They guide you through every cough and splutter of the application process (and make it sound incredibly complicated!); give details about the selective exams; tell you how they allocate places; tell you how to appeal a decision; inform you about waiting lists and lots of other general information such as what to do if your child has special needs.

Some brochures also publish a sample application form (known as the Common Application Form, or CAF form) so that you know what information will be required when you fill it in.

Bear in mind before reading the Bexley, Kent and Bromley brochures that they're not really published for your benefit. They're aimed at parents who live in the borough and want to send their child to a school in the borough. There is however, always a section for people who live out of the borough and want to apply. Because of this **you MUST obtain your own local authority's brochure – for e.g. Greenwich or Lewisham. Your local authority is who you pay your council tax to. You may not wish to go to any of their schools, but you have to apply through them. They co-ordinate your case and they send you the offer of a school on March 1st.** Read it extremely carefully and do not expect them to automatically send it to you because you're a resident of their borough – they don't, you have to actively seek it out.

### Open Days/Evenings

An open event is one of the best ways to get a feel for a school. In my experience this counts for a lot. It can be a bit like buying a house – you walk in and just know it's right. Most of the grammars hold several events over several days at several different times to ensure everybody who wants to go can do. However not all do. Newstead, for example, holds just one (on a Saturday) and it's absolutely packed. There's always a long queue to get in and forget parking nearby because it's chaos.

The headteacher speaks at most events – but not all. Check with the school beforehand to make sure, because what they say – and the way in which they say it – does help you form a view about the school and its ethos.  It's likely that you will be given a tour of the school by a pupil, or a couple of pupils. This is an invaluable opportunity to find out from the horse's mouth what it's really like to attend the school. Ask them questions that address issues you may have concerns about and try to ask interesting/obscure/probing questions that may enlighten you on subjects that *really* matter. The likelihood is that the pupils will answer truthfully but, if they don't, it will probably be obvious. (I guess loyalty to the school is a good thing!) Don't place too much importance on the quality of the tour. If the children aren't born tour guides it doesn't mean the school isn't good. Having said that, the way in which they and their peers handle the tours and the way in which they interact with you and other people could, in my opinion, be an indicator of the general behaviour and attitude in the school.

Finally, try to walk into an open event with an open mind. Forget your pre-conceptions and what your friend's cousin's sister-in-law said about the maths department. Find out for yourself and trust your instincts.

## Talking

Talk to as many people as you can, but mainly those who have a child at the school, used to have a child at the school, or those with personal experience of the school (for

35

e.g a governor, dinner lady or a visiting sports coach).
Other people's opinions and experiences can be immensely
helpful, particularly if they're people like you or have a child
like yours. Ask them straight questions and request straight
answers. If you're worried about your child being bullied ask
them if they know of any bullying incidents and, if so, how
the school dealt with them. (From about Year 4 onwards,
secondary school transition and the 11-plus are the most
talked about subjects at the school gates. Get involved if it
makes you happy, but my advice is to limit your
conversations. Don't get drawn into the twice-daily
playground parent forum on the subject because it will
probably make you more anxious than you already are –
particularly if Perfect Parent X seems to know everything
and it makes you feel you know nothing.) Talk to your
child's teacher and headteacher. Although they do not know
your child personally like you, they know more about them
educationally and their perspective and opinions may often
be different to you own. They may also have 'inside
knowledge' about the schools you are considering. Many
have been in the job years and have a honed insight into
what the schools are really like and what sort of child they
really suit. Bear in mind though – particularly where
headteachers are concerned – that they might just have an
agenda. Some headteachers of primary and secondary
schools form informal coalitions whereby children are
pushed towards a certain secondary school for a reason you
are not privy to. Talk to your child too. It's quite likely that
they know something about a school from their friends who
have got it from a brother or sister who attends the school.
Word of warning though; be aware it could be no more than
playground gossip.

# STEP 3

## FIND OUT WHAT EACH EXAM ENTAILS - AND MAKE SENSE OF IT

Life would be simple if each education authority's exams were the same, but they're not. **THEY'RE ALL DIFFERENT.**

Here is what each one sets:

**BEXLEY**
Verbal reasoning (75 questions in 50 minutes)
Maths (50 questions in 50 minutes)

BOTH PAPERS ARE MULTIPLE CHOICE
The exams are held on two separate days at a school within the borough. The location changes most years. Likely to be a weekday.

**KENT**
Verbal reasoning (80 questions in 50 minutes)
Non verbal reasoning (72 questions in 40 minutes)
Maths (50 questions in 60 minutes)
Writing (a choice of essay titles – 60 minutes) this is not marked and is only used in the case of a headteacher review if the pupil fails the test.

ALL PAPERS – APART FROM WRITING – ARE MULTIPLE CHOICE

The exams are held one after the other on the same day at a school within the borough. Unlikely to be nearby. Likely to be on a Saturday. Often an early start – e.g 8.30am.

## **BROMLEY**
Verbal reasoning
Non Verbal reasoning.
(It's actually the two schools – Olave's and Newstead – who set their own exams, rather than the authority)

St Olave's is: English (comprehension and writing) and maths.
One hour each. Maths 30 questions (of increasing difficulty). NOT MULTIPLE CHOICE.

Newstead is: Verbal and non verbal reasoning.
Verbal is 85 questions in 45 minutes

Non verbal is 80 questions in 40 minutes (broken down into four ten minute sections. i.e 20 questions per 10 minutes)

BOTH MULTIPLE CHOICE

The exams are held one after the other on the same day at the school whose exam you are sitting. Likely to be a weekday in September which is earlier than the other grammars.  Often an early start – e.g 8.30am.

# Verbal and non-verbal reasoning. What on earth do they mean?

Reasoning tests are designed to identify potential academic ability. They test whether a child can problem solve, whilst working quickly and accurately, and how effectively they can process information.  As an adult they are more generally known as logic or psychometric tests. They are sometimes used as part of a job interview process.

Reasoning tests: a mystery to most people

## VERBAL

Verbal reasoning focuses on words. They can be broken down into four sections: sorting words; selecting words; anagrams and coded sequences. The sub-categories of each are as follows:

### Sorting Words

Find words that have letters in common
Find an opposite word
Identify groups of words
Pair up words
Sort words into categories
Find words that do not belong
Find words that are most similar

<u>For example</u>:

> <u>Question -</u> Select two words (one from each group)
> that are similar –
> (liquid, soft, fixed)  (rough, fluid, melt)
> (sing, melody, music)  (laugh, instrument, tune)
> (dear, customer, buy)  (expensive, gift, present)
> <u>Answers:</u> liquid/fluid, melody/tune, dear/expensive

## Selecting Words

Finish one word and begin the next
Make compound words
Transfer letters to make new words
Make new words by adding letters
Make new words by removing letters
Find a prefix for a set of words
Choose pairs of opposites

<u>For example</u>:

> <u>Question  -</u> Move one letter from the first word and
> add it to the second word to make two new words
> (in any order)
> Plume   rat
> Feather   head
> Stick    no
> <u>Answers:</u> plum/rate, feather/head, sick/not.

## Anagrams

Find a small word in a larger word
Find a word hidden in a sentence
Rearrange letters to make a word
Rearrange a sentence to make sense of it

Use a rule to create new words
Crosswords
Put words into alphabetical order

For example:

> Question - Find the missing three letter word that
> must be added to the other letters to create a
> correctly spelt word
> Answers: HOE (shoes), WEE (sweets), OUT (trout).

## Coded Sequences

Code and decode words with the use of symbols
Code and decode words with the use of numbers
Code and decode words using letters
Make deductions from given information
Work out letter and number sequences
Apply number logic

For example:

> Question - Sally, Sue, Sam, Steven and Seb are
> 10,9,8,7 and 6 years old but not in this order. Work
> out who is the youngest from these clues.
> Steven is 1 year younger than Sam
> Seb is older than Sally
> Sue is 2 years younger than Sam
> Sally is 2 years younger than Sue
> Answer: Sally is the youngest

# NON VERBAL

Non verbal reasoning focuses on patterns and shape rather
than words. They test whether a child can problem solve

while working out quickly and accurately - and how effectively they can process information though graphic or pictorial representation.  But what does this mean in practice? Non-verbal reasoning tests can be broken into four categories: Identifying Shapes; Missing Shapes; Coded Shapes and Rotating Shapes. The sub-categories are as follows:

### Identifying Shapes
Identify shapes and patterns
Recognise shapes that are similar
Pair up shapes

### Missing Shapes
Find shapes that complete a sequence
Find a missing shape from a pattern
Find a given part within a shape

### Coded Shapes

Code and decode shapes  using numbers
Code and decode shapes using letters
Apply shape logic

### Rotating Shapes
Relate shapes to nets
Link nets to cubes
Recognise mirror images


# MATHS

11-plus maths focuses mainly on topics covered in the school curriculum up to Year 6. They can be broken down into four sections: Number logic; Shape and Size; Graphic

Data and Number equations. Sub categories within those sections are as follows:

## Number logic

Applying number logic
Using negative and positive numbers correctly
Using mean, mode, median and range
Understanding probability and ratio
Making numbers squares
Understanding Number Lines.

For example:
Arianna Jackson gives her four children pocket money each week. She hands out a total sum of £20 and divides the money in relation to the ages of the four children.  Lisa is 16, Tracy is 14, Simon is 12 and Troy is 10. The pocket money is given out 1:2:3:4 with the largest portion to the eldest child and smaller amount to the youngest child.

Question - a)How much pocket money does Lisa get?  b) How much pocket money does Tracy get? c)How much pocket money does Simon get? d) how much pocket money does Troy get? And e) what is the average amount.

Answers  a) £8  b) £6  c) 4 d) £2 and £5

## Shape and Size

Movement of angles
Finding, size, perimeter and volume
Understanding vertices, faces and edges
Recognise shape, symmetry and rotation.

For example:
Question -  Which of these shapes has at least once pair of parallel sides?

a) Regular pentagon
b) Rhombus
c) Trapezium
d) Isosceles triangle
e) Regular hexagon

Answers:   b,c and e

## Graphic Data

Understand co-ordinates and compass points
Understand conversions
Use graphs, charts, tables and decision trees
Work out scale and dimension

For example:

Look at this timetable and answer the questions:

| | High St | Wood End | The Banks |
|---|---|---|---|
| **Lodge Road Terminus** | | | |
| **Bus A** | 09.14 | 09.20 | 09.50 |
| 10.03 | 10.15 | | |
| **Bus B** | 10.00 | 10.06 | ------ |
| 10.30 | 10.42 | | |
| **Bus C** | 11.20 | ------- | 11.45 |
| 11.58 | 12.10 | | |

Question:

a)  How long does bus A take to get from High St. To the Terminus?

44

b) How long does it take from Lodge Road to the Terminus?
c) What is the quickest time from Wood End to Lodge Road?

Answers:

    a) 61 minutes
    b) 12 minutes
    c) 24 minutes


## Number Equations

Use addition and subtraction
Use division and multiplication
Understand multiples of numbers
Work out Fractions and Percentages
Recognise equations use prime, square and cub numbers

For example:

Question - Underline the odd one out:

a) 9     16    25    81    101
b) 0.1   0.25  0.5  0.75  1
c) 25%  50%  75%  80%  100%

Answers -
a)101
b) 0.1
c)80 per cent

# STEP 4

## BE PREPARED!

**Founding father of America Benjamin Franklin once said:** *"By failing to prepare you are preparing to fail."*

And he was right.

Being bright or a high achiever does NOT guarantee you a place at a grammar or selective school – FACT.

You need to be able to pass the entrance exams – and in some cases (for e.g if you live miles away from the school of your choice in Bexley) you have to pass them exceptionally well.

Unfortunately, they do not necessarily favour the most naturally bright children, they favour children who understand the specifics of the tests and can do them well. This is particularly true for verbal and non verbal reasoning as they are not taught at school.

I know of a child who was quite bright but not bright enough to be in the top sets at school for literacy or maths. However, they just had a knack for verbal and non verbal reasoning and, with the additional help of a tutor, managed to get into one of the super-selectives which sets both the exams.

For everyone else it's quite simple and like anything else you don't know how to do, you have to learn.

Then, you have to practice, and practice, and practice, and practice some more...get the picture?

Bear in mind this will have to be done out of school in your child's own time. Very few state primary schools in south east London help with the 11+. This is due to the fact that pupils are not expected to take it as there are no selective schools in the boroughs. As a result, the education authorities discourage their headteachers from providing any assistance within school. For obvious reasons town hall bosses would prefer that bright children stay schooled within their own borough.

Interestingly, however, a handful of heads ignore this and introduce what's often known as puzzle practice - usually in Year 5. Puzzle practice is a type of code name for verbal and non verbal reasoning practice, the idea being that the pupils may not fully appreciate what they're practicing for and feel like they're having a bit of educational 'fun'.

This can, however, be controversial, as some parents who are not considering sending their child to a selective school object. Because 'puzzles' are not part of the national curriculum they do not believe it is not in their child's best interest to be doing them.  Others think the school is pandering to the needs of pushy middle class parents who often tend to be more vocal in terms of what they request of the school.

It's a tricky one for heads. It seems that those who have a pushy parent clientele often oblige. In other cases, if it's a high achieving primary school, the head genuinely sees it as something necessary as he or she knows that many will end up taking the 11+ regardless.

Be aware, however, that even if your child does puzzle practice at school, the level tends to be a lot lower than the

11+ itself. Also, they do not get 'taught' how to do the puzzles, it's simply a chance to practice.

## When?

Knowing when to start your preparation process is a difficult one. Many pushy parents believe the earlier the better. But, if you've got little George or Georgina doing verbal reasoning practice papers after school in Year 2 or 3, then that is definitely too early and you are - to put it bluntly - robbing them of their childhood.

It is, of course, a matter of personal preference, but I suggest your decision should be influenced by one or more of the following factors: a) what you consider your child's ability and potential is b) how your child is likely to respond to extra work c) existing homework commitments d) existing sports and leisure commitments  d) your availability.

The 11+ grammar school exams take place at the beginning of Year 6 (mainly in October). The 11+ entrance exams for independent schools take place in the January of Year 6.

**In my opinion, a good time to start is at the beginning of Year 4.** Bear in mind the earlier you start the more gently you can take it and, hopefully, the less pressure you will have to exert on your child. Most people would agree, however, that you need at least 12 months to do a proper preparation job. Less than that and you might find yourself panicking, not to mention your child.

In order to make the most of whatever time you've chosen, you should draw up a plan of preparation – maybe even in the form of a timetable.

Your child doesn't have to see this (it could terrify them), as long as you know what's going to happen – and when - as it will be your job to see it through.

A word of warning on this matter, it is highly unlikely your child will welcome extra work. Few children at ages 9 or 10 are driven enough to always want to do what it takes to get desired results. They may well be able to aspire to something; they may well have the intellectual sophistication to understand what this means in terms of commitment, but on a day to day basis there will always be something they would rather be doing than extra work. I promise you!

So, it's a good idea before the whole process starts to sit down with them and have a chat. If they don't already know, explain why it's important to go to a really good secondary school and tell them straight why this means having to take a test (at this stage use the word 'test' rather than 'exam'). Describe why the test does not primarily concentrate on the subjects they learn at school and why it's necessary, therefore, to do so some work out of school to learn the new topics. Point out, however, that maths features in all the exams (all except Newstead Wood, that is) and they will be a need to put in some extra work on that too.

Once you've picked your child up off the floor, assure them that they won't be in it on their own, that you'll be with them every step of the way. Say you believe in their ability and that they deserve to go to a really good school. Present the situation as a wonderful opportunity rather than a cross to bear. Tell them you love them; tell them you'll get them that new Playstation game they want. Tell them whatever you need to in order to get them on-side. There is no point starting the extra work if your child doesn't think (in principle at least) it's a good idea.

**Explain about the extra work then pick them up off the floor**

### Types of Preparation

**Self Help Books**   There are hundreds on the market about the 11+. Go into the educational book section of any WH Smith (or similar) and you will see them all lined up. It's difficult to know which to pick because many of them seem so relevant and your instinct is to buy as many as possible to give your child the best chance possible. But as they cost between £7 and £10 each, you need to be practical and decide what's most suitable at the time you happen to be in the shop.

To make it easy for you, the first one I would recommend you buy is called: *The Parents' Stress-free Guide to the 11+.* It is published by the most prolific 11+ publisher Bond and it gives you an invaluable overview of everything you need to know about the 11+ generally; the specific exam topics (with examples and explanations of how to do them); the exams themselves and what happens afterwards. Obviously it is not geared to any particular locality and is far less useful than this guide (!) but the 11+ principles are much the same wherever you go. Usefully, its chronological order doubles-up as an introductory preparation structure which you can adapt to your circumstances. This is what I did anyway, and found it worked.

Some of the books available cover more than one topic, some focus on verbal reasoning, some on non verbal, others on maths, others on English. Some explain in great detail how to do various things – like, for e.g a particular type of verbal reasoning question. Others, focus on short exercises where there's an explanation of the answer. Most of them have a recommended age range (for e.g 9-10 years) which I advise you pay special attention to as it's very easy to pick up the wrong one.

The main publishers to look out for are: **Bond, Letts and GL assessment**. Their content is most relevant and their examples and practice tests mirror the 11+ questions your child will face most closely. In fact, it is GL assessment (formerly known as nfer Nelson) which is used by the vast majority of education authorities – including Bexley and Kent – to set their entrance exams. Other lesser known 11+ publishers include Bright Sparks and AFN.

### Practice papers and 'Ten Minute Tests'

In the same section of bookshops like WH Smith you will find row upon row of short tests and practice papers. The main publisher of test papers is GL assessment which produces numerous different packs of four papers. Some just contain one subject and others are 'variety packs' for e.g one maths, one English, one verbal reasoning, one non-verbal reasoning. These are not age graded because they assume if a child is ready to practice for the test, then the questions are appropriate. As well as the practice papers these packs contain answer sheets (for the multiple choice format tests) and notes for parents with instructions on how to complete each test, plus answers.
Although practice doesn't always make perfect, it certainly helps. Practice tests also help familiarise children with the style and format of the 11+ paper making the real tests less

scary on the day. When your child is confident enough, make them tackle the tests under timed conditions. This helps them manage their time effectively which means, hopefully, on the day of the test they'll do the same.

Practice papers are also important because they paint a picture of your child's strengths and weaknesses, giving you a clear understanding of what help they require. And, if your child is lucky enough to be achieving good scores in them, this can really boost their confidence in the run up to the exams. Conversely, if they're not scoring well, they can be de-motivating. So, make sure you don't present them with a test paper too early.

Practice papers are more expensive than the books. You will have to pay at least £10 for a pack of four. Do not be afraid to do papers more than once, though. Record the date and your child's score and then go back to the same paper, say, a month later and see if they've improved. It's also a good idea to chum-up with your children's friends' parents who are probably also buying these papers. Swap with them and then someone else and you'll save yourself a lot of money.

The 'ten minute' tests are similar to papers, only they're contained in a book and they're obviously a lot shorter. Children warm towards them because they know they won't take long and they're less intimidating than an exam-style document. They're an effective tool to use before you move on to practice papers.

**Specimen Papers/Questions**

These are documents that give examples of questions that have been set before. **Bexley publish specimen papers on their website. Kent does not have any. Newstead sell them for £5 and St Olave's publish them on their website**. Do get them, because they show the style and academic level expected for a particular school's test. You will note if you compare them, there are differences.

### 'Fun' Activities

Anything that is fun and makes learning effective is a good tool in preparation for any exam, particularly the 11+. Skills required to do verbal and non verbal reasoning questions can be improved by doing things like **crosswords, word puzzles, Suduko, jigsaw puzzles and board games such as Scrabble and Yahtzee**. There are also many websites which have a range of educational games that can help to. Try: bbc.co.uk/school/games or www.11plusknowledge.co.uk (free for a month). See back of book for more.

# STEP 5

## TO TUTOR OR NOT TO TUTOR, THAT IS THE QUESTION

**...and the simple answer is YES**

The education authorities and secondary schools dislike coaching of any kind and specifically warn against professional tutors. They argue that the 11+exams are designed to reveal innate ability, skills, habits and potential rather than specifically acquired factual knowledge. They say there is little point tutoring a child to pass an exam as this is not a true representation of their ability. Furthermore if, as a result, that child ends up in a school that is too academically challenging for them, they will suffer in the long term.

Maybe...

But everyone's doing it which leaves you at a distinct disadvantage if you don't.

It's sad fact of selective school life. Competition for places is such that it's advisable to do everything you can to secure one of them. If tutoring happens to be one of those things (which it is) then so be it.

In an ideal world, no one would hire a tutor and the 11+ exam would be a level playing field. But, it's far from an ideal world where education and opportunity is concerned and you've got to play the game to have a chance of winning it.

Remember, being bright and intelligent is not necessarily enough to get you into a grammar/selective school. You need to be good at passing exams. And, that's where a tutor comes in.

A tutor cannot make an unintelligent child clever. A tutor can, however, teach a bright child specific skills which can help them pass an exam. Ironically, the child may therefore appear brighter. But you do need to decide whether this is appropriate for *your* child. The education authority is right about one thing: there really is no point getting your child into a high achieving school if they're going to struggle from start to finish. They will be miserable academically and socially and the chances are they will under-perform as a result.

Luckily, there is evidence that tutoring works. A 2004 study in Northern Ireland (Bunting and Mooney) showed that "coaching by tutors can significantly boost attainment at 11+. 500 students were asked to complete a number of tests – with some given tuition beforehand. Just three hours of extra help was shown to have a 'significant' effect on attainment – and this effect became 'substantial' after nine months of tutoring.

- So, how do you go about finding a good one? Well, **word of mouth is best**. There are a handful of established individuals in the Greenwich/Lewisham area and if you don't know who they are, you can bet one of the people standing next to you in the playground does. So, ask them. (Data protection prevents this Guide from revealing their identities). Expect to pay at least £30 an hour to a tutor whose home you go to. More, if they come to you.

Then there's **tutoring companies** which provide on-site 11+coaching. Many of them offer initial assessment, taster courses, on-going study, holiday refresher courses, pre-exam 'crash' courses and mock exams. They normally offer group lessons in addition to one to one coaching. One such firm is called YES Tuition in Greenwich. Others are local branches of national franchises such as Kumon. Costs vary, but expect to pay at least £30 for a 90-minute group session, £40 for a personal one. Some companies require a deposit as a deterrent against missing lessons in addition to a registration fee of around £30. A full assessment of a child's abilities can cost £150.

And **schools** – only some private ones though - offer after-school and weekend 11+ courses both in group and one-to-one form. For example in Blackheath, Heath House School and Blackheath High School for Girls do it. The cost tends to be a little higher than tutoring firms.

And **tutoring agencies –** many of whom have numerous tutors on their books whom they are happy to put you in touch with. But in my experience very few of them are clued-up about the *local* 11+ system. They tend to be general tutors who may very well be able to assist you, but the sessions may not be geared towards the types of exams your son or daughter will be sitting which, to my mind, is key if you're serious about success. Inevitably a tutor employed via an agency will be more expensive because the agency charges a fee. An example of such as agency is Fleet Tutors.

**Online tutoring** may be of use, but as you do not get one-to-one time with a human being their benefits are limited. They provide information, advice, tutorials and online 'papers' which are marked as you go. When you get a question wrong, you get an explanation of how to do it correctly. You then get another question in the hope that you've learned. Feedback is often done via a parent's email. Some sites give free 'demos' so you can try them out before buying. Be warned, they're not cheap. My advice would be to use these websites as an additional learning tool. One such established website site is www.bofa11plus.com (see back of book for more)

And lastly:

**When Should you Start tutoring?**

Well, it is one of those things that's down to personal preference (not to mention how anxious you are!) but my advice is NOT at the beginning of your child's overall preparation. So, if you decide to start that at the beginning of Year 4, I would suggest waiting at least a year before you include a tutor in the mix. In my experience the important thing is NOT the amount of time you have a tutor, it's the quality of the tutoring and your child's ability to take it on board and develop it at home.

Some people choose to tutor their child themselves throughout. In my opinion this is a risky strategy unless you have an unusually co-operative and bright child, plus you have the abilities and patience of a proper tutor. Research shows that children do learn academically better from people who are independent of their domestic situation – which is one of *many* reasons why there are so few home schooled children. A mother I know chose to go down the 'tutor-your-own-child' route and says she will regret it for the rest of her life. Along with her daughter's grandmother they took it in turns to tutor the bright but shy girl. The mother's expectations of how the girl would do in the tests had been raised by the school and she thought her decision was a sensible and loving thing to do. It wasn't. The girl failed most of the tests she took – including a re-sit – although she did manage to get into a private school which, luckily, her parents could afford. But the woman told me afterwards she would always live with the guilt of making her daughter feel like a failure and that she felt one too.

I know of another case of a average intelligence child who was sent to a well known tutoring company from the beginning of Year 2. She just scraped though the Bexley test and got assigned one of the sought after mixed grammars. A couple of months into Year 7 she stopped doing her homework, wasn't achieving well and had made almost no friends. She was flagged up as a problem and her parents were contacted to discuss the matter. The first question they were asked related to how much and how long the child been tutored for the 11+ (the inference being she'd only got into the school because of it) The parents were unhappy at the line of questioning and the subsequent suggestion that she might cope better - and be happier - if she changed schools and went to a comprehensive. It was pointed out to them – and it maybe of interest to you – that the education authority does not have the power to remove a child from a school on this basis, but they have a responsibility to advise strongly on what they believe is in the child's best interest. The parents ignored the suggestion and dealt with the matter privately. A few months down the line, the child is now thriving, has some friends and is a lot happier.

# STEP 6

## ADMIN

Have you ever wondered why an anagram of 'admin' is: 'a mind'? No, well here's my theory: you need a good mind (a really organised one to be precise) to appreciate why admin is so important – and never more so than where 11+ organisation is concerned.

You may well be considering schools from more than one borough. In fact, if you want to increase your chances of getting into a grammar school, you definitely will be. If you're going for the super-selectives in Bromley as well as schools in Bexley and Kent, you will be dealing with the admin processes of three different organisations. And, if you're going for independent sector too, then you must add their systems to your organisational equation.

Whatever your scenario they'll be a lot to do, a lot to sort out and a lot of deadlines to be met. They'll be telephone calls to be made/logged, emails and texts to be sent and papers, letters, brochures, prospectuses etc to be filed. So, you need to be organised. You need to be on top of the admin, otherwise it will get on top of you. Maybe even engulf you.

My advice is to set aside a little area where all your 11+ paraphernalia can go. If you've got room on a surface by your computer, then that's obviously a good place. (under the printer table was mine) Buy A4 files and label them accordingly: Bexley, Kent, Olave's/Newstead and

Independents. Label others as you wish but 'tuition' 'Greenwich/Lewisham' 'general' will probably come in useful. Then, as and when you acquire things like a letter from an education authority, put it in the respective file. Then buy something like magazine files for all your school prospectuses, brochures and general literature and arrange the whole shebang neatly. Ensure it's out of the way but accessible. Remember this little set-up will be with you for many months and you really don't want it dominating your room (not to mention your life!)

Label a notebook "11+" in which you only write down things to do with the process. Take it with you on school visits etc and use it when you speak to someone on the telephone. Underline anything important in red pen.

You could even put up a year-planner-style wall chart where you timetable everything you need to do by a certain date.

I know these suggestions are pretty obvious. But you would be surprised how many people don't act on the obvious and end up in a right mess. For example, I know of someone who would have missed a deadline for registering for an exam had I not reminded them – simply because they were busy and not very organised.

So, once you're set up in a physical sense, the next step is to do the essential administrative tasks that will enable your child to actually sit the exams. The first one is:

60

Get organised

## Registration

All the grammar and Independent schools have a date by which you must register your child to take the exams.

For **Bexley** schools, it's usually between **the beginning of May and mid July.**

For **Kent** schools, it's usually between the **beginning and end of June.**

For Newstead and St Olave's there is a one-date deadline for registering for the tests. It's currently **July 6** for both.

**\*All of these dates relate to the same year of the exams. As the precise dates can change every year, you are advised to double-check them for yourself.**

Registration can be done online or through the post with Kent, but for Bexley it must be done on paper and posted. For Newstead/St Olave's it must be done by submitting a supplementary information form either in the post or in-person. The schools recommend in-person in case it goes missing. (more about supplementary forms later)

**Bexley's website** is: www.bexley.gov.uk/admissions and their email address is: SelectionTests@bexley.gov.uk. (general queries) However you must get and return a hard copy of the registration form which can be done by: telephoning 020 8303 7777 option 6, emailing: customer.services@bexley.gov.uk or you can download and print one from the webpage www.bexley.gov.uk/selectiontests

**Kent's website** is: www.kent.gov.uk/ola and their admissions email address is: kentonlineadmissions@kent.gov.uk should you wish to call for a hard copy of the form the telephone number is: 01622 696565

Each Independent school has their own deadline for registration, but they're normally towards the end of November. Be aware that almost all of them require a (non returnable) registration fee, usually in the region of £60.

## **Supplementary Information Form**

This is an additional document that must be submitted to some schools as part of your registration/application process.

As the name suggests, it asks for supplementary information such as: whether or not your child has a sibling already at the school; has your child got any Special Educational Needs and has your child ever sat the selection test before. They are used for admin purposes only.

Currently, **none** of the **Bexley** grammar schools require one.

**Dartford Grammar School for Girls DO require one, as DO Wilmington Grammar School for Girls.**

Both **Newstead and St Olave's require one.**

Once you have registered for the exams you will receive confirmation and a reference number from each organisation. Keep this bit of paper particularly safe in the unlikely case of problems.

# STEP 7

## <u>MOTIVATE YOUR CHILD, DE-STRESS YOURSELF</u>

**'Never think the sky's the limit when there's footprints on the moon...'**

Repeat this to your child this and see what they say! Find out if they understand it and, if they don't, attempt to explain its profoundness.

And then...return to Planet Earth and make some outlandish promise to get them something they want if they work hard for the 11+!

Yes, bribe them if you have to. I say this tongue in cheek but with an element of seriousness. What I really mean is that you *have* to find a way of motivating your child to do the extra work – preferably with a good grace – because it's unlikely they'll actually want to do it. So if your child happens to react positively to incentives (as most children do) then in my opinion this is as good a starting place as any where motivation is concerned.

You might be thinking bribery is NOT the way to go and that your child should understand there's no gain without pain and that the 'prize' for hard work will be a place at a fantastic grammar school.

And maybe you're right, but be realistic. Children are not wired to think like adults and cannot truly appreciate the virtue of delayed gratification. They need something a bit more tangible to get them going. So why not the stick and carrot approach?

A small gift at the end of the week - if they've worked well – is one way of going about this. If you view it is as a *reward* for good behaviour rather than a bribe, then I promises that you will feel more comfortable about it (the system is really no different to the star chart you probably had for your child as a toddler)

And surely it's better to reward than punish?

Be careful what sort of gift/treat you offer/give them though. Make it SMALL. (save the new phone for when they actually get into the school!) It is important that your child realises what they get is just a token of your appreciation and a bonus for them doing extra work. For example, a cheap paperback book, a set of pens, a bracelet from Claire's for the girls, a pair of football socks from JD Sports for the boys. Alternatively, little treats like having a friend round for a sleepover, going to the cinema, a meal out or an afternoon ten-pin bowling are probably 'cool' enough to work.

Remember, however, there's no point having an incentive scheme unless you stick to it. If your child has a tantrum when asked to do a maths paper and you have to bundle them to their desk, then NO prize that week. And, if your child is constantly making the same silly mistake because they can't be bothered to check their work, then NO prize that week. It's easy to give-in believe me, but don't, just tell yourself you're being cruel to be kind...

The thing about motivation is that sometimes you need it more than at other times.

If you decided to start your child's 11+ preparation very early at the beginning of Year 4, say, then you've got a two year period in which you've got to keep them focussed and driven. That's not easy. Maybe at the start of the process your child will be enthusiastic and upbeat. Bright children tend to enjoy the challenge of a new project. Maybe as the exams approach they'll knuckle down because they know have to. It's the period inbetween where it can be tricky.

For the record, I do not think you should introduce the incentive scheme when your child first starts the extra work. Initial work should be gentle and not goal orientated. At first *you* should be very involved by way of going through things with them – just like a tutor would. The self-help books are very useful for this because they take you through the natural chronological order of a particular topic. So, even if you don't fully understand it, it's explained on paper and your child probably will (in the event that neither of you understand it, then find someone who does!)

You may not have had yourself down as a teacher, but in the first instance that's what you need to be. You must plan what they're going to do that day/week/month, go through it with them and then set them work on it. When they've finished that work you need to mark it, and if they've got some wrong answers you need to go through them ensuring they understand where they went wrong. Then, set a couple more questions. Only when you're positive they understand the topic, should the lesson end. Be sensible though, if things are not going well and it's 90 minutes since you started, just stop and go back to it the next day. If would be counter-productive to continue because your child would become tired, un-cooperative and demoralised and that would not help motivation.

In fact, in my view, none of the sessions with your child should go on for longer than an hour. Half an hour is more than sufficient if they've got the hang of something. Don't work them seven days a week either. It's too much.

And, when you go away on holiday give them a total break from work. Maybe a little revision while you're away as the exams approach is a good thing, just don't overdo it. Remember how old they are and remember what a holiday is meant to be about – a break from work.

By the way, don't worry about your ability. You don't need to be Brain of Britain to do any of this; you don't need any training either. Just acquire appropriate material, digest it beforehand, try to understand it, and then be a Mum/Dad. You've taught them hundreds of other things that you were not an expert on, and the 11+ work is no different. The bonus is that you'll be surprised how much you can recall from your own school days and you'll be buoyed by the fact that you'll be picking up new skills yourself (honestly!)

In the early preparatory stages it is important to reassure your child of your full support, love and belief in them. Remember, if *you* believe in them, then hopefully they'll believe in themselves in times of doubt. Make it clear, however, that you too are committing to all this but, in order for it to work, it must be a two way thing. I recall telling my daughter on numerous occasions that I would not *allow* her to go to a bad secondary school. (I had no idea how I would accomplish this if she failed the exams by the way!) but that there would be absolutely nothing I could do about it if she didn't work hard and she was allocated a bad comprehensive school. It certainly made her think...

Motivating your child is one thing, but what about motivating yourself? Bet you hadn't thought of that!

Well, that's simple; your motivation *is* your child. You want what's best for them and you'll do what it takes. That's what being a parent's all about (isn't it!?)

Don't be under any illusion it will be easy for either of you though. There will be times when neither of you want to sit down and bury your head in a book. And, on the odd occasion when this happens, then DON'T! Motivation is about what works for you and while I would not advocate this approach very often, the chances are the next time you sit down, both of you will be more enthusiastic.

Commitment and consistency will help keep you motivated and should enable you to motivate your child. It's an on-going process, but once the extra work becomes part of a routine, it won't feel like extra work, it'll feel like the norm, and then motivation will be less of an issue.

Just keep on the case and know when to push, when to coax, when to shout, when to whisper, when to laugh, when to cry, when to reward and when to punish. You'll be Bad Mum/Dad; Good Mum/Dad; Sweet Mum/Dad; Sour Mum/Dad; Happy Mum/Dad; Sad Mum/Dad; Proud Mum/Dad; Disappointed Mum/Dad etc etc.

And you'll be Busy Mum/Dad; until you get a tutor - at which point you'll be Relieved Mum/Dad!

## STRESS (and how to have less of it)

I know of an intelligent, middle class former high-flying career woman who nearly drove herself to an early grave due to anxiety and stress over the 11+. She had, of course, started preparing her daughter for it ridiculously early – the middle of Year 2 if I remember rightly - and soon after gave up her well paid job to concentrate on it. For her, the 11+ was a project and failure was not an option. She had adopted this attitude in her professional life and it had always worked; she saw no reason why the same approach couldn't be applied to her daughter and the 11+.

By the beginning of Year 5 she had been spotted in the street more than once weeping and whereas before she had been a sociable, immaculately dressed proud sort of woman, she soon changed into a fairly shabby recluse who, if you made eye contact with her, looked like a rabbit caught in the headlights.

People who knew her worried. They asked her what was wrong but she always denied anything was. Friends' husbands had a quiet word with her husband to see if there was anything they could do, but he was a very guarded person and told them they were fine. Granted, this woman was busy and clearly feeling the strain of having other children; but everyone knew it was more than that. And the reason they knew, was because every time anyone spoke to her, her ONLY topic of conversation was the 11+. Not only was it her only conversation, once she started talking about it she just couldn't stop. In fact, she would work herself up into a near-frenzy when discussing things that she was anxious about. And there were lots and lots of things she was anxious about but they all added up to the same thing: what would she do if her daughter didn't get into a grammar school?

Quite simply for her, it would have been the end of the world and she would have blamed herself entirely.

She confided in one person that she had become completely obsessed with the whole thing and that she couldn't sleep at night because of worrying. Matters had been made worse because the family no longer had the safety net of a private school option because money had become tight since she stopped working. At one point, she said, they were thinking of selling the house in case it came to having to pay school fees.

The woman went to her GP for help. He prescribed Temazepam. One day she took an extra tablet in order to get a little sleep during the day while her children were at school. It worked and she slept. In fact she overslept and woke up 20 minutes after pick-up time. Horrified and dazed, she jumped into her car and without thinking reversed out of her drive and...BANG slammed straight into another car which was coming round a corner. Luckily she only suffered whiplash but she was badly shaken and if the other car had been moving faster and at a different angle, the outcome could have been a lot worse.

This was a wake up call for the woman and with the help of a counsellor she managed to calm down by the middle of Year 6.

Unfortunately it was too late for her daughter. Inevitably the stress had already been passed-on and before of one the exams she was so nervous it was touch and go whether she would actually sit it or not.  In the end she did and, I hasten to add, got into a grammar school (though not the one the mother had set her heart on) So, there was a happy ending of sorts, but the process through which the whole family had to go to get there was far from happy and the strain nearly broke them.

I tell you this story as a warning. Do NOT become this woman. While getting your child into a really good school is important it should not take over your life. More importantly, it should not take over your family's life. So, don't neglect your other children; don't neglect your husband/wife/partner and don't neglect yourself. You are more than just a 11+mum/dad and you deserve a separate existence.

Too much stress is counter-productive anyway. It makes you snappy, miserable and tired which is no good if you're trying to help your child with work. And projecting your own anxieties onto your child is a really bad thing. In worst case scenarios it can stay with them for the rest of their lives, not to mention 11+ exams. So, if you are stressed, try to keep a lid on it. You do not want your child stressed too. It will not help them pass exams and that, remember, is what your stress is all about...

**Do not become this woman!**

Things that you can do to avoid your child becoming stressed include: not constantly talking about the 11+ and secondary schools; not comparing them with their friends and classmates; not pushing them too hard; reassuring them that as long as they do their best you will be proud of whatever exam results they get; and encouraging them to be open about their feelings; and when they have concerns talk things through with them - and then give them a big hug.

If you think your child is stressed though, you must deal with it. Symptoms to look out for include: withdrawal, tearfulness, moodiness, change of appetite, weight loss/gain, insomnia, mystery aches and pains, tummy problems, inexplicable sickness and a sudden worsening of existing conditions such as asthma.

In the first instance, talk to them about it and give them a break from work. Re-assure them daily of your love and support and explain that while the 11+ is important it's not as important as their well-being. Go and see their teacher and/or headteacher to let them know of what's going on. Give them time, give them space and give them whatever it is they psychologically need. If after a couple of weeks there's no change, then make an appointment with your GP.

In summary, while it is completely understandable if you or your child is stressed, my advice is to try to regulate it by keeping the whole 11+ thing in perspective. Compared to having a healthy, happy child, what secondary school they end up in does, somewhat, pale into insignificance doesn't it?

Get your priorities right: having happy, healthy children are more important than getting them into the 'right' school.

# STEP 8

## THE EXAMS

A few weeks before the exams you will have been sent confirmation that your child is entered. The letter will contain basic information like the start time and the test location.

Newstead and St Olave's hold the exam on their premises, but for Bexley and Kent you will be allocated a school within the respective boroughs. Do not expect the Kent one to be nearby. Kent is the largest education authority in the country and it is possible that your test site will be 40+ miles away. In 2011 most children from Greenwich and Lewisham had to travel to Tonbridge (30 miles away) for an 8.30am start. Yes, 8.30am which means a lot of children got up around 6am in order to leave at 7am in order to ensure enough time in case of traffic problems etc. The nearest possible location for the Kent test is one of the two Dartford  grammar schools.

Bexley's easier because the majority of the schools in the borough are closer. Having said this, you have to attend two exams on two separate days, so you've got twice the anxiety of getting there in time!

As anyone who has ever tried to get anywhere in and out of London knows, traffic and public transport are often a complete nightmare and you can never guarantee you'll be somewhere at a particular time. So, for exams, my advice is to leave more than twice the amount of time you would normally need to get there. In the case of Kent, if the test centre is anywhere like Tonbridge, I would honestly recommend booking into a hotel or bed and breakfast nearby the night before. I did this and knowing that I was on the doorstep gave me immense peace of mind. It also meant my daughter didn't have to get up at the crack of dawn, unlike her friends – some of whom looked tired before the exam started.

And plan your route. It's likely you'll be going to places you've never been before and you need to make sure you know not only *how* to get there, but the *best* way to get there. So, do a dry run. Whatever mode of transport you plan to use, use it on the test run and take notice of potential hazards that could affect your progress – for e.g long term roadworks on the M25.

And, if you're going by car - particularly down an A-Road or motorway - you may wish to consider going in convoy with another family. This means that if one of your cars breaks down, the other can take your child to the test.

All this is important because if you miss the exam that's it – grammar school dream over. Only unless there are exceptional circumstances (such as your child breaking an arm on the day) will you be given another date to sit it.

**Practice Makes Perfect**

One good thing about the **Kent** test is that your child gets the opportunity to do a mock one first. Everything is just as it will be for the real one – including the location, start time etc. The only difference is that the 'writing' paper is not included and the other three tests are not marked. It normally takes place exactly a week before the real one and although it's not compulsory, my advice is to do it. Not only is it a great chance to practice under proper exam conditions, but it should put your child's mind at rest on the big day because they know what to expect so it doesn't feel so scary. Do not be surprised, however, if the papers at the practice tests are ones your child has done before because they're available to buy in shops. This happened in 2011. In my opinion it would be a lot more use if this wasn't the case because finding the questions familiar - and therefore easy - can lull a child into a false sense of security leading to misplaced complacency for the real thing.

**D-Day**

Practice test done; make sure the night before the exam your child gets to bed early. I do not advise revising at this stage due to the fact that if they haven't got the hang of something by now, it's a bit late.

Before you leave home on the day, make sure your give them a generous breakfast – preferably something healthy and nutritious that slow-releases energy for e.g porridge, banana and wholemeal toast with a topping. And do not forget liquid. A drink with their breakfast along with a bottle of water to take with them is crucial. The body needs to be properly hydrated in order for muscles (one of which is the brain) to work efficiently. Once you've checked to make sure they've got the required things in their pencil case – pens, pencils, rubbers, a ruler and the slip of paper confirming they're entered into the exam – you can leave the house.

On the journey to the test centre chat with your child about anything other than the exam, it will only make them nervous otherwise. The exception to this rule is re-assuring them that they will be fine and that they're sufficiently prepared for the task ahead. Remind them that you love them and that all you expect is that they do their best.

Maybe even give them something to look forward to immediately after the exam – for e.g lunch in a place they like. Before you let them go, encourage them to go to the loo and remind them to locate the clock in the exam room to enable them to make time checks during the test (wearing a watch too is a good idea)

A word to the wise: the day of your child's first exam may feel surreal. You've been preparing them for this moment for months (years maybe) and now it's finally here the outcome depends entirely on a few pencil marks and biro scribbles on an answer sheet (see picture). The enormity can be overwhelming and the loss of control unsettling. The bottom line is it's all down to little George or Georgina who, until recently, you couldn't trust to tie their own shoelaces!

You'll be scared, you'll be panicking and you'll not want to let your child go. If only you could do the exam for them. If only you could come back another day. If only the rest of their life didn't depend on the next couple of hours. If only you'd never had a child then it wouldn't feel like *you* were staring into an abyss right now!! Yes, your thoughts will be racing, but pull yourself together and remind yourself it's not your exam. Remember, the last thing your child needs is the projection of your own anxieties onto them. Ironically they're probably a lot calmer than you. Not only are children more focussed that you think, it's highly likely that they'll be standing around with their class mates talking excitedly about the new app they've downloaded.

So, let them go – both physically and metaphorically – and find yourself a nice coffee shop in a nice shopping centre where you can chill-out for the next couple of hours. The good thing at this stage is that there's nothing more you can do. Your work is done, it's down to them now and I can't tell you how good (as well as terrifying) that feels!

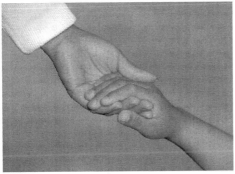

**Let them go physically and metaphorically**

Afterwards, do what comes naturally - ask how it went and how they feel they've done and then leave it do not go on and on about It, they will have had a belly-full already. Don't stop them talking to their friends about it, but it's not a good idea for them to start comparing answers in case someone suspects they've done badly because their answers were different to their pal's.

Then get on with your day. If you've planned something nice for them, do it and if you haven't, just carry on as you normally would. Although you know it's a big deal that the first exam is over, you really don't want your child to feel that way because it could pile on the pressure for the next one.

Depending on how many exams your child is doing, by the time the last one arrives you'll probably be feeling a little more chilled out – as will your child. That's good but not as good as the feeling you and your child will get when they're all over! Put simply, the relief is IMMENSE.

For the first time in months (maybe years!) you will relax. Two days after my daughter's exams finished we went on holiday. We got a bit of sun, sand, rest, relaxation and a complete change of environment and perspective. All thoughts of the 11+ disappeared and we concentrated on having fun and doing things totally unrelated to work. If felt

77

like another world – because it was – and it was helpful to lose ourselves in it. You don't have to go on holiday to achieve these things but doing something totally different for a while is a good idea.

Bear in mind your lifestyle with inevitably change from now on as it won't be necessary for your child to knuckle down to out-of-school work all the time. Even if you think it's sensible to carry on with *some* extra work just to keep them on their toes, make sure you give them a LONG BREAK before you re-start, they deserve it.

# STEP 9

## <u>THE MARKING, THE RESULTS AND WHAT TO DO IF IT ALL GOES PEAR-SHAPED</u>

Be aware the results do not take long to arrive. In fact, you've got less than a month before you start stressing again! Bexley's are issued on or around **October 12th** and Kent's follow on or around **October 17th**. As previously mentioned, Newstead will, for the first time in 2012, issue results before the schools application form has to be in, but for St Olave's you will not know how your child has done until March 1st when your local authority will inform you if your son got in. If he didn't, you won't even find out how he did because St Olave's don't send you the test results (unlike Newstead used to). However, if you call or write to them, they will tell you.

**Bexley's** are issued by letter in the post. You find out the individual scores for maths and verbal reasoning out of **140** and the total score out of **280**. You are informed what the pass mark was (be aware they don't call it a pass mark) and you are told whether your child has been 'deemed selective.' What this means is whether you child has passed the 11+ and is eligible to be considered for a grammar school place, or not.

**In 2011, the pass mark was 218.**

In the same year **4862** children sat the selection tests and **1394** were deemed selective. You don't need to be a whizz at maths to work out that that's not far off 75 per cent of pupils who 'failed.'

**Kent's** are issued online if you have registered online and then in the hard copy in the post. By post if you registered by post.                          All you find out from them in whether your son or daughter has been deemed selective (i.e passed the 11+). If you want the scores you have to ask your headteacher or pester Kent County Council who, in my case, seemed quite reluctant to hand them over.

Crucially, **the Kent test can only be passed if your child achieves a minimum score in each test** (except writing). In 2010 it was **117** (out of **140)** in **2011** it had gone up to **119**. So, if your child is gifted at, say, maths, but very weak at, say, verbal reasoning then they could fail because an exceptionally high score in one subject has no bearing on a very low score in another. In this sense, to pass the Kent test you have to be a very good all-rounder.

**Standardised Scoring**

A controversial subject for some, the marking for ALL 11+ exams is adjusted slightly to allow for a child's age when they take the test. This is done through a complicated statistical process called **standardisation** which ensures that a child's results are compared with other children of the same age. It means that a child who was born in, say, late August and takes the test when they are just 10 does not suffer at the hands of a child who was born in, say, early September and takes the test when they are 11. In this example if both achieve the same initial score (known as **raw score**) the younger child's standardised score will be higher than the older child's. It is, however, only the standardised score that counts.

There is another variable that standardisation deals with: the fact that the number of questions on a test paper and time allowed nearly always differs to another one. For e.g if a non verbal reasoning paper has 80 questions in 50 minutes while a maths paper has 100 questions in 45 minutes, simply adding the raw scores together will not give equal weight to the results of both tests, and nor will an average. Standardisation is a way, therefore, of giving equal value to the results of each test, regardless of the number of questions and the time given. This way, all the tests can be marked out of 140 and compared.

The complicated statistical process used to calculate a standardised score really is so complicated that few people understand it! The truth is, you don't really need to. Suffice to say marking is done on an automated machine and specialised computer software is used to create a reference table called a 'look-up-table for each test paper. The minimum standardised score is derived from the look-up-table which lists both the raw scores of each pupil and their age in years and months. The actual number will vary depending on the average score of those taking part and the number of applicants.

The following facts should make it more real for you:

**For the Kent verbal reasoning tests in 2010:**

To achieve a standardised score of **120** at age **just 10**, the child had to score 36/80 (45%)
At the age of **10 years and 6 months**, the child had to score 39/80 (49%)
At the age of **11**, the child had to score 42/80 (53%)

So, that's a **8%** 'handicap' for an 11-year-old compared to a 10-year-old.

To achieve a standardised score of **140** at the age of **just 10,** the child had to score 58/80 (73%)
At the age of **10 years and 6 months**, the child had to score 61/80 (76%)
At the age of **11**, the child had to score 63/80 (79%)

So, that's a **6%** 'handicap' for an 11-year-old compared to a 10-year-old.

This illustrates why the system is controversial and why some people resent it. As you can see, there can be a significant difference in the outcome for two children who score the same before their result is standardised. For obvious reasons, critics of the system tend to be parents with older children in their year. The way they see it is that their child is penalised for being on the Planet a little longer than another child in the same class who has been taught exactly the same things throughout their school life. Again for obvious reasons, parents with younger children tend to support standardised scoring. They point out that their child has been slightly less developed over their school life and that the 'handicap' system takes this into account.

My daughter was born on September 2, so you can imagine where I stand on this!  A word to the wise: If you're reading this before conceiving and you want to know the best time to give birth, (in terms of 11+ outcome) my advice would be February or March, that way your child is at neither end of the standardisation spectrum...Extreme advice maybe, but if you plan to be a pushy parent, then you may wish to take it on board.

## What to do if your child fails the 11+ but they shouldn't have done

Firstly, break the news to them gently and comfort them until they're consoled. It is likely they will be devastated (as you will be) and there could well be bafflement with regards what went wrong. The point is, you'll never find out because the education authority will not discuss any aspect of your child's test with you.

I know of children who came out of the Bexley test in 2011 declaring how easy it was who then failed, while those same children came out of the Kent test claiming it was 'really hard' and passed.

So, you can't rely on your child to explain what happened, so there's little point asking them. I know of a girl who was expected to walk the Bexley test, but she failed. Her mother was upset and a little annoyed because she became convinced that the girl had done something stupid like miss out an entire page of the exam. Her reason for thinking this was that the girl came out of one of the tests claiming it was 'easy' and that she'd finished in just 20 minutes - a third of the time given for the test. This made her mother concerned and suspicious because it seemed too good to be true. She knew her daughter was bright – but not that bright. So, when the results came through, in one sense the failure was not a complete shock. The mother contacted Bexley to see if she could get any feedback on the result. She also asked if she could be told if her daughter had missed out a page. The answer to both questions was 'no'.

The first thing NOT to do is panic if all the evidence suggests your child should have passed the test (evidence such as how they performed at school in similar tests, how near they were to the pass mark etc).

Then, ask your headteacher if he/she will formally request a **review**. *This only applies to **Bexley** though.*

The review has to go through the headteacher, not you. If the headteacher believes your child's score accurately reflects their ability, they may turn down your request.

What happens then is that the headteacher puts together a dossier of information that indicates the test score was not an accurate reflection of your child's ability and submits it to Bexley. The panel set up by the authority then looks at it and if, for whatever reason, they agree the child's mark is unfair, they have the power to give the child the chance to re-take the exam. A new date is given, the child sits it (a different paper) and the new results are sent out over the Christmas period.

If, this time, they are deemed selective they are eligible for a grammar school like anyone else. Parents in this position are still advised to put any Bexley schools they are interested in on their Common Admission Form (which must be submitted before the retake results) though it is a somewhat risky strategy because if the child still fails the re-take, then the Bexley schools on the form ware automatically wasted preferences. If you find yourself in this position, I would advise only putting your favourite one or two Bexley schools on the form.

**Kent** does it differently. Before test results are sent out to parents they are sent to headteachers. If the headteacher believes a child who has failed the test should have passed, he or she can submit evidence to the authority for a review. It is at this point that the writing exercise each child did in the test comes into play. It is considered independent evidence of the child's ability. If the panel appointed believes that the child is of grammar school calibre, they change his or her status from 'non-selective' to 'selective' and when the results go out to the parents they simply see one of the other. As Kent does not reveal test scores unless specifically requested, nobody – apart from the headteacher – knows what's gone on. It should be noted that the headteacher is obliged to keep it private.

Newstead Wood and St Olave's do not have reviews because admission is simply based on rank order in the tests.

**If it all goes pear-shaped don't panic**

# STEP 10

## THE CAF FORM

The full name for the CAF form is the **Common Admission Form.** Some people ironically refer to it as the *Choices Are Frightening* form because it's where you make crucial decisions that will affect the rest of your child's life (no pressure then!)

Transfer from primary to secondary school is not an automatic process that magically happens - even if your child passes all their exams. You have to apply. You do this by filling in what's called a CAF Form and submitting it to your local authority (the one you pay council tax to). This can be done in two ways, either online or on paper.

It's best to do it online because the system is quick and easy to use; it's open from September 1st until the closing date 24 hours a day, seven days a week; there's no risk that your application will get lost or delayed in the post and you will receive almost immediate confirmation that your application has been submitted successfully. Perhaps the main advantage, however, is that when the results come out on March 1st you will be notified the same evening online whereas people who have filled in a paper form have to wait for the post to arrive.

All London authorities are signed-up to the Pan-London Co-ordinated Admissions Process and to apply online there is ONE website address for everyone. It is:

# www.eadmissions.org.uk

After logging on, you first you need to register and create a password and account. Once you've done this you're automatically linked to your local authority and you're ready to go. You can dip in and out of your account at any time and edit information as you wish.

If you want to apply on paper and live in Greenwich and your child goes to a Greenwich school, then he or she should be given one at school. If you live in Greenwich but your child goes to another authority's school – e.g Lewisham, then you have to obtain one yourself. This can be done via the council website: **www.greenwich.gov.uk/admissions** or by telephoning **020 8921 8043.**

If you live in Lewisham and your child goes to a Lewisham school, then he or she should be given one at school. If you live in Lewisham but your child goes to another authority's school – for e.g Greenwich, then you have to obtain one yourself. This can be done by telephoning **020 8314 8282**.

If you apply online, do not also complete a paper form and vice versa – it WILL cause confusion although the online one will take priority.

The form itself looks quite long and complicated, but it's not really. It is however important to take care filling it in, because mistakes could affect the school your child is offered. Each authority's form is very slightly different but the fundamentals are the same. The following information is required from everyone:

*Full details of your child, including what school they go to and their permanent address.

* Parent's details – from the person who is filling in the form who must either have sole or shared parental responsibility for the child.

## * School Preferences. This is the big one!

In this section you are asked to name up to six schools that you would like to apply to. Schools must be ranked in order of preference. You must only list state schools and this includes schools from outside the borough where you live.

So, for people like YOU whose children are aiming for a grammar school, it's possible that NONE of your listed schools will be in the borough where you live. Don't worry, that's OK, your application is forwarded to the relevant local authority or school as appropriate.

Some people whose child is expected to get into a grammar school still choose to put a favoured comprehensive school within their borough on their list as a sort of safety net in case the grammar schools on their list are oversubscribed and cannot offer a place. These people feel that if this happens, at least their child will end up in a school they find acceptable. In fact, most education authorities advise you to do this. Whether you choose to or not somewhat depends on your personality. Optimistic risk takers don't, cautious pessimists do. Which are you!?

Deciding your preferences is one of the most difficult aspects of the whole 11+ process. By the time you come to fill in the CAF form, you will have the results of the Bexley and Kent tests. So, at least you know whether you're eligible to list a grammar school or not. Until 2012 you were not told the results of the Newstead or St Olave's test which meant that putting either school down on the form could be a wasted preference if you hadn't got in but didn't know it. That situation remains with St Olave's but not Newstead. For entry in September 2013 you will know whether your child has been offered a place, or not, before filling in the CAF form. This does of course make sense and everyone wonders when St Olaves' will follow suit.

So, this is the point where all your research, school visits, talking to people etc comes to the fore and by this stage you should really know which schools you're going to put down and their approximate order.

Although you should have already studied it, as I have yet to mention **admission criteria** – more commonly referred to as **oversubscription criteria** where popular schools are concerned - then this is the best time to do so.

ALL the grammar schools are oversubscribed. This means they all have more applications than they do places and some people who want to go will not be able to.

**To illustrate this, here are the figures for the 2011 intake (the applications relate to 1st-6th preferences)**

**Chislehurst and Sidcup Grammar School**: **1051** applications,  **192** places

**Bexley Grammar School**: **1089** applications, **192** places

**Townley Grammar School for Girls**: **338** applications, **210** places

**Beths Grammar School: 635** applications, **160** places

**Dartford Grammar School for Girls**: **718** applications, **150** places

**Dartford Grammar School**: **753** applications, **150** places

**Wilmington Grammar School for Girls**: **623** applications, **120** places

**Newstead Wood: 872** applications, **135** places (there are now 160 places)

**St Olave's**: **847** applications, **112** places.

There is only **one way to guarantee yourself a place at a grammar school – and that's by coming in the top 180 pupils in the Bexley Test** (in terms of highest total score) If you achieve this, you can choose which Bexley grammar school you go to and you would then put it at the top of your CAF form.

For everyone else (who passes the tests and is deemed selective) it is each school's oversubscription criteria that dictates whether you are offered a place or not.

The trick is, therefore, to study each school's criteria and work out how that might affect your child's chances of getting in. Then, you can strategically decide where to place the school on your CAF form.

For **BEXLEY** the criteria are as follows and are the same for all four grammar schools:

1) Children in care
2) Top 180 in test
3) Medical (if the child has a condition which means it is **essential** to attend a particular school
4) Sibling (i.e if a sibling already attends the school at the time of admission)

5) Distance (priority given to those living nearest the school based on the measurement along the shortest public walking route)

For **KENT**, each school has its own criteria, as follows:

## Dartford Grammar School for Girls

1) Children in care
2) Siblings
3) Girls living within a mile of the school
4) Girls living in the borough of Dartford or one of the following parishes: Ash-cum-Ridley, Bean, Crockenhill, Darenth, Eynsford, Farningham, Fawkham, Hartley, Horton Kirby and South Darenth, Longfield and New Barn, Southfleet, Stone, Sutton at Hone and Hawley, Swanley, Swanscombe and Greenhithe, West Kingsdown and Wilmington.
5) All other eligible girls seeking a place ranked in the following order – those performing best in the Kent Test and, in the case of tied scores, preference is given to the child living closest to the school.

## Dartford Grammar School for Boys

1) Children in care
2) Boys living in the following electoral wards: Brent, Bean and Darenth, Castle, Heath, Joyce Green, Joydens Wood, Littlebrook, Newtown, Princes, Stone Sutton-at-Hone and Hawley, Town, West Hill, Wilmington.
3) All other applicants regardless of address (in the case of tied scores, preference is given to the boy living closest to the school.

## Wilmington Grammar School for Girls

1) Children in care
2) Sibling at school
3) Sibling at Wilmington Grammar School for Boys
4) Girls who came in the top 12 for maths in the Kent test
5) Distance between home and school

## Wilmington Grammar School for Boys

1) Children in care
2) Sibling at school
3) Sibling at Wilmington Grammar School for Girls
4) Boys who came in the top 12 for the Kent Test
5) Distance between home and school

So, as you can see, unless you have another child at a grammar school or your child happens to have done exceptionally well in the tests, the main criteria for your consideration is the distance between your home and the schools you favour. To put it bluntly, what this means is that the further the school is from your home, the less chance you have of getting into it.

And I can tell you from my experience and knowledge, that if you live in the borough of Lewisham or certain parts of Greenwich such as East Greenwich, West Greenwich, Westcombe Park and Woolwich it is more difficult to get into the following schools than the others: Bexley Grammar School, Chislehurst and Sidcup Grammar School and both the Dartford Grammar schools.

Greenwich is a big borough, though, and its borders are near Bexley, Kent and Bromley, so, if you live in Eltham, say, you've got far more chance of getting into one of the schools listed above because you're geographically closer.

Newstead and St Olave's have one simple criteria: those who do best in the test. (so, for e.g, Olave's has 112 places and they go to the top 112 performers) In the case of tied scores for Newstead, preference goes to the higher scoring child in the later stages of the non verbal test. For St Olave's it goes to the higher scoring child in the maths test.

Only one of these two schools has a geographical requirement: for Newstead you have to live within a 9 mile radius of the school based on an ordnance survey map calculation. This covers most of Lewisham and Greenwich

On March 1st, you will be offered just **ONE** school. The **order of preference** in which you list the schools is therefore really important. If more than one school can make an offer, the system will simply select the one that is ranked highest on your CAF form. So, choosing your rank order for the CAF form is not just about what school you'd like your child to go to, it's about how sensible it is to put a school in a particular position on your form if you know your chances of getting in there are slim.

I know of several people in Greenwich and Lewisham who wanted their child to go to Bexley Grammar which is around 5 miles away. They were aware, however, that because of where they lived it was unlikely that they'd get in, but they still put the school as their number one preference. This was foolish because it was a wasted preference. Had they looked at Bexley's own brochure which devotes an entire section to 'home to school distance' they would have seen that the previous year the maximum distance for which a place was offered was 3.8 miles. Although the distances change from year to year, as applications for grammar schools are rising, that distance is likely to reduce, rather than increase, giving such applicants almost 0% chance of getting in.

I know of another case where someone who lived around 4 miles away from Bexley Grammar put it as their first choice school despite entering their son into the highly competitive St Olave's test. The reason this person did this was because although they (and their son) dreamt about going to St Olave's, they knew how difficult it was to get a place, so they put it at number 2 on their list. They thought they were being realistic. To their surprise he did get in and was allocated the school. However, think about what would have happened if, for some reason that year, Bexley was able to offer places to people who lived four miles away. Yes, he would have been allocated Bexley Grammar and would have missed out on his dream school Olave's.

Interestingly, Townley Grammar School for Girls (in Bexleyheath) is a high achieving well respected school which, in 2011 were ranked higher than most of the other grammar schools for GCSE and A-level. However, despite it being further away geographically than, say, Bexley Grammar, it was able to offer a place to EVERYONE who applied there.

Why? Who knows? That was the education authority's answer when I put this question to them! Clearly one of the reasons is that they have more places to offer than some schools and considerably fewer applications. Also, as a single-sex school, boys are automatically removed from the application equation. But, even that doesn't make sense because normally the higher achieving schools attract more applications. The trend does more or less coincide with a long-established female headteacher leaving and a new male one arriving...but the truth is it could just mean that there are anomalies within the system that are inexplicable and might faze you when deciding on your preferences, but don't let them put you off. Go with your instinct coupled with copious research, data analysis, historical perspective and good old commons sense.

**Always list six schools on your CAF form** even though you don't have to. Clearly it increases your chances of being offered a school that you in some way favour. If, for example, you only list three or four there's certainly no guarantee that you will be offered one of them and you may well end up with a school that you hate.

I know of someone who was trying to get their daughter into a grammar who only listed three schools in the belief that because there was a sibling policy at the popular local comprehensive and they already had a son who was thriving there, if their daughter failed to get into the grammars then at least she could go to a school round the corner they were happy with. Trouble is, she didn't get into either of the two grammars and then after submitting the CAF form her brother was bullied and the parents withdrew him. This meant at the time of admission she did not have a sibling at the school and whereas she had originally been offered a place on the basis of that, it was withdrawn and she ended up at another comprehensive school about three miles further away that her parents had not wanted her to go to.

So, let this be a warning – put six schools on the form, don't waste a preference.

Don't think that the order in which you list the schools will affect your chances of being offered a place in terms of competition between the schools. No school is told about other schools on your list, or the order in which you've placed them. The order of preference is simply used where it is possible to offer a place at more than one school.

Other frequently asked questions include: **If I list a school as my first preference, does it mean I have a better**

**chance of getting a place than someone who lists that school lower down their list?**

The simple answer is **NO** as each preference is considered on its merits using the admission criteria for that particular school.

And: Am **I guaranteed a place at one of the six schools on my list?**

The answer is **NO**. In 2011, **146** out of **2,821** Lewisham children did not get a place at any of the schools on their CAF form.

However in reality most people who have made realistic choices do get offered one of their six but it all depends on how many people have applied for a place that year, the order in which they have listed schools and where they live. Be aware that what can also happen in reality is that you have listed six schools but don't really want your child to go to the bottom one or two – and it's one of those you're offered. If this happens you have a problem. Apart from appealing or requesting that you go on another school's waiting list (more on this later) there's not a lot you can do.

And: **What if I don't submit my CAF form by the closing date?**

The closing date is **October 31st**, although everyone is encouraged to submit their form before the start of the half term holiday which normally falls around **October 21$^{st}$ or 22$^{nd}$**. If you do submit late but before **December 16** for Greenwich and Lewisham it will still be accepted and included in the main process in time for an offer to be made on March 1$^{st}$ – but only if there is a **very good reason.** Very good reasons might include the death of a close relative, or where a family has just moved into the area.

Evidence of the reason for lateness will be required. Where the reason for lateness is judged not to be good enough or it is received after December 16th the application will only be considered AFTER offers have been made – in which case you've got almost no chance of getting the school you want.

There are slight differences in the questions that are asked on CAF forms depending on your local authority. Greenwich asks for more information than Lewisham does. In fact one of the last sections on the Greenwich form is a real pain because when you get to it you assume you've almost finished and then realise you haven't because you are asked to list your child's: **ability band and Year 5 optional SATS raw scores for reading, maths A and Maths B. Alternatively you can list their National Curriculum Levels in reading and written maths**... Now unless you're really up to speed on every aspect of your child's attainment, then you probably can't answer these question without consulting your child's teacher/headteacher. So do this, but if you're up against time don't worry too much. The reason for asking these questions relates to streaming at comprehensive schools and as you're hoping your child will attend a grammar school the information might not be needed at all. I know of someone who left this section blank and there was no come-back because the child got into a grammar school.

Once you've submitted your form you will get confirmation it's been received and a reference number. If you've done it online and you change your mind about something on the form before the closing date, you can go back and revise it as many times as you wish, only the most recent version will be the one that's considered.

At the time of submission you will be reminded if any of the schools on your list require a supplementary form. If they do, then you need to submit that to the school as part of a **dual application**. Without the form, the school cannot consider your request for a place.

Once you've done all this, you simply have to wait for March 1 to find out what school you've been offered. It will feel like the longest four months of your life!

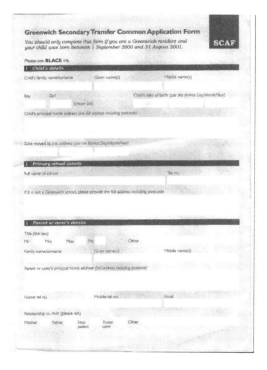

The CAF form looks complicated but it isn't

# STEP 11

## MARCH 1<u>ST</u> – NATIONAL OFFER DAY – AND ITS AFTERMATH

"March comes in like a lion and goes out like a lamb."
Latin proverb

I think **National Offer Day** sounds like a public holiday. I happen to think it should be made into one, but only for the parents who haven't slept for a week as they wait to find out what school their child has been offered.

The wait is horrible but, like death and tax demands, it will arrive – and when it does you might wish it hadn't due to the rate at which your heart is pounding!

If you submitted your CAF form online, your offer will be emailed to you at around **5pm**. If you supplied a mobile telephone number you will receive a text alerting you. If you did it on paper, you will have to wait for the post.

The email comes from the Pan-London e-Admissions systems team and you have to read down to paragraph 5 before finding out your school. (If I was in responsible, I'd put it right at the top in big, bold type...) The letter comes from your home authority.

Remember, you only get offered **one** school.

Hopefully it will be one of your top preferences. If not, at least one of your six and, if not, a school that means you won't have to emigrate!

If you haven't been offered your number one school, the email/letter will advise why – in a general sense - and you will be told what the closing date is for a reply – normally **March 15<sup>th</sup>/16<sup>th</sup> Take** note of it and remember to RSVP.

So, now you know what school you've been offered, you can decide what to do about it. Undoubtedly you will have considered the various potential scenarios and will probably know instantly whether you want to accept it, or not. There are **surprises with offers** though. While some are predictable (for e.g if Townley was your number one preference and you lived nearby, then you're as good as guaranteed to get in) but others are unexpected and some are downright shocking.

For example, I know of a family who were quietly confident their daughter would get offered Dartford Grammar School for Girls because a family who lived in the same road had a daughter who got in two years before. They were, however, disappointed to find they were offered Wilmington Grammar School for Girls which is a lower-achieving school and awkward to get to because of its semi-rural location. They told their daughter they were happy, but they weren't (and neither was she).

Another family whose son passed both the Kent and Bexley tests were devastated to discover that despite putting both authorities' schools on their CAF form; they were offered the local comprehensive.

So expect the unexpected and have a contingency plan.

### Waiting Lists

If you've been offered one of your first two or three preferences I would respectfully suggest it might be foolish not to accept it – particularly if it's a good grammar school. However, you can accept the place AND request a place on the waiting list of a higher preference school/s which is what a lot or pushy parents do. You can also do this if you've not been offered *any* of your preference schools. Unless there are exceptional circumstances your child cannot be added to the waiting list of a lower preference school than the one you were offered.

Once you've made your request, your child's name will be added to the school/'s waiting list ranked in admission criteria order. If a vacancy arises (normally due to someone else turning down a place) the place will be offered to the next applicant on the list – hopefully you. If you don't accept it, it will be offered to the next person on the waiting list and so on.

At the beginning of the new school year if your child is still on the waiting list of a school, you will be asked if want to remain on it. If you do, you must confirm in writing.

After the new school year starts, spaces at the school will only become available if a pupil in Year 7 leaves and the number of pupils falls below the school's admission number. In that case, the place would only be offered to a child whose parent had requested they stay on the list and were next in line.

**Bexley'**s waiting lists stay open until the end of the first term of the school year.

**Kent's** remain open until July 6.

Newstead and St Olave's have their own waiting lists which you can request to go on. When Newstead send out your daughter's test scores you are given an indication of your approximate likely place on the list for e.g "greater than 100". As St Olave's do not send out the scores the only way you can decide whether there's any point going on the waiting list is to contact the school and find out your son's rank order. Let's face it, if he came 650th just forget it...

## Appeals

Under the Schools Standards and Framework Act 1998 you have the right to appeal against the decision not to offer your child a place at any of the schools for which you've applied. You can appeal to as many as you like.

You make your appeal to the admission authority of each individual school (for e.g for Chislehurst and Sidcup Grammar school it would be Bexley and Wilmington Grammar School for Boys it would be Kent). Details of what exactly you have to do are included in your offer letter.

The authority sets up an Independent Schools Appeal Panel which consists of three to five members of the public, some of whom have a particular interest or expertise in education. None of the members had anything to do with the original admission decision and they have no connection with the school to which you are appealing.

The following is a summary of the **procedure and protocol**:

1) You must submit the appeal in writing setting out the grounds on which it is made. Include any documentary evidence you believe helps your case, (for e.g if your child has a health problem which means they cannot walk far and you want them to attend the nearest school to your home because of it, then a medical report from a doctor confirming your child's physical limitations is likely to be of help.)

2) You are entitled to attend the Appeal with the child's other parent and, if you wish, another person who could be a friend or even a legal representative

3) The main matters which the Appeals Panel must take into account are: the preferences expressed on the CAF form, the arrangements published by the Admission Authority and your reasons for appealing.

4) The Appeal is held in private, sometimes at a town hall, sometimes at a school. There is meant to be an informal atmosphere to put you at your ease. Sometimes the head teacher of the school your appealing against attends, sometimes it's a representative of the authority.

5) The Panel asks you questions, based on your reasons for appeal, and will often probe further into your answers.

6) You are entitled to ask questions yourself of both the panel and the representative.

7) If the panel decides your case is stronger than the school's it will uphold your Appeal and award your child a place at the school.

8) The Appeal decision is pretty quick, normally within 7 days. It is binding on the admission authority and

the school's governors. It can only be overturned by a court.

I speak from (successful) experience - at primary school level - when I tell you there is a lot of work involved in an Appeal and you should not take it on lightly. You must gather as much evidence as you can to support your case and this might take time, effort and lots of research. However, there is help out there. Numerous books have been written on the subject and there are firms and organisations which specialise in assisting people such as **The Advisory Centre for Education (ACE). Their website address is: <u>www.ace-ed.org.uk</u> and their Freephone number is 0808 800 5793.**

Be aware, also, when considering an Appeal that **most of them fail.**

**<u>The 2011 figures for grammar schools in Bexley alone speak for themselves</u>:**

Bexley Grammar School – 10 heard, 10 failed.

Chislehurst and Sidcup Grammar School – 3 heard,  3 failed

Beths Grammar School – 13 heard, 13 failed

Townley Grammar School for Girls – 1 heard, 1 failed

• In 2010 some Appeals *were* successful

Most authorities require that you lodge your Appeal by **March 19th,** although Greenwich's date is **March 30th**. They must write to you at least 10 school days before the hearing to confirm the date. All Appeals must be heard before **July 6** (of the same year)

If you're unhappy about the way in which the Appeal process was carried out you can complain to your **Local Government Ombudsman**. While they can recommend a new Appeal the Ombudsman cannot review or overturn the panel's decision.

If there is a change in your circumstances you may be able to Appeal more than once - if the admission authority considers the change relevant to your application.

Hopefully come the start of the new term in September when your child's all grown up, smart and ready to leave the house, they'll be heading for a school that you - and they - are happy with.

If they are, then all the hard work, stress, tears and tantrums will have been worth it.

If they're not, put a brave face on it so you don't pass on your disappointment, and think carefully about what you may wish to do next.

I suggest you do nothing for a while. See how they settle in, see how they do academically and see if they like the school. Remember things change; good schools can go bad and bad schools can come good. It's also possible that what all headteachers say could be true – that a child who wants to do well  and is prepared to work hard will thrive whatever school they're in.

And if you remember nothing else, remember this: school is important – very important – but it is only one part of your child's life and they actually spend less time there than they do at home. Support behind closed doors is therefore crucial to every aspect of their existence and without it they may never fulfil their potential - academic or otherwise.

# THE INDEPENDENT SECTOR

You might be thinking there's no point reading on because you can't afford private school fees which average out at around £14,000-a-year in London.

Neither could I, but my daughter is now attending a private school so...

THINK AGAIN!

I never planned to go private, it just worked out that way because having gone through the whole 11+process within the state system, it struck me that there was nothing to lose by my daughter doing some independent school's 11+ exams too.

I knew that many of them had a range of financial incentives on offer – like academic, sports and music scholarships which are awarded on merit regardless of parental income, not to mention means-tested bursaries which, for some people, can mean that 100 per cent of the fees are waivered.

So I thought we'd have a go. Luckily my daughter passed the exams well and I was offered a financial package – including an academic scholarship - at more than one school that made it possible to choose which one she went to. I could not believe my good fortune and was incredibly grateful to the headteachers who made the offers.

My daughter's state school offer was at a high achieving all-girls' grammar school which I would have been very happy to accept if the private school project had not worked out.

Anyway, it worked for me and it could work for you – if you think a private school would suit your child, that is. My advice is: don't rule it out before you've ruled it in.

If money is the over-riding issue, find out which local schools have the most to give away! I'm serious, and here's a bit of guidance: if you're the parent of a high achieving girl and you want them to go to an all-girls school, then I suggest you start with **James Allen's School for Girls** in Dulwich. If you're the parent of a high achieving boy and you want them to go to an all-boys' school, then consider **Eltham College.** If you've got a boy or a girl and you want them to go to a mixed school, then **Colfe's** in Lee should be your first port of call.

Each of these schools encourages applications from the parents of high achieving children who would be interested in joining the school but wouldn't consider applying because they can't afford it. However, such schools are equally keen to attract the high achieving children of those who *can* afford the fees because bright children play a big part in what makes a school successful nowadays (think league tables/university places etc)

Some independent schools are in a position to set aside vast amounts of money to entice pupils they want. It's no secret how they operate and there's no shame in taking advantage of it. In the case of one school I know there is approximately £140,000 to give away each year. This figure roughly equates to 10 places at the school for 12 months. It's divided up as the headteacher sees fit and includes academic, sports and music scholarships which are only

awarded to the highest performing in each category and means-tested bursaries for those on limited incomes.

**Some schools seem to be made of money**

On the subject of scholarships, when you fill in independent school registration forms you will be asked if you want your child to be considered for ones including sport, music and art. You will *not* be asked if you want them to be considered for an academic scholarship, because everyone *is* automatically.

My advice is: if your child has any particular skill in any of the scholarship subjects, then enter them. You have nothing to lose and everything to gain. Don't worry, they don't need to be gifted at something in order to be awarded a scholarship, if they're good at it, then they're in with a chance. I was incredibly surprised by the number of children familiar to me who were awarded scholarships for things that they were not well known for being good at.

And, the fact is, if you can't afford all the fees, but you can afford part of them, then a scholarship – which is awarded on a % basis, up to a maximum of 50% - can be your way in.

It's reassuring to know that scholarships are awarded for the child's academic life (up to the sixth form anyway). Bursaries, however, are means tested and are reviewed every year. So, if you were unemployed when the bursary was awarded and then you won the Lottery, you *would* be liable for the fees!

If your child is shortlisted for a scholarship they will have to attend an interview. The academic interview is normally with the headteacher or the deputy. Sports scholarship interviews take the form of having to compete in a number of sporting disciplines. For music, you have to play pieces on your favoured instrument and for the art one you have to produce a portfolio of work.

If money is not the over-riding issue for you, then all your child has got to do is pass the school's entrance exam and they're in – well as good as. Almost all the independent schools interview the child as a matter of course. Don't panic, it's not a scary interrogation; it's more of an informal chat in order to give the school a flavour of your child. Questions range from things like: 'who is your favourite author? and 'what subjects do you like at school' to 'what sports do you play' and 'why do you want to come to this school?' (a word to the wise: tell your child NOT to say their favourite author is Roald Dahl, Jacqueline Wilson, Michael Morpurgo or Anthony Horowitz that's whom all children say and it makes your child look like a clone. Remember, one of the qualities independent schools look for is individuality)

Some schools place more importance on the interview than others. For e.g I know of one school which interviews *before* the child even takes the exam which somewhat negates its importance due to the fact they could fail and not even be eligible for admission. I know of another where how the child comes across in the interview has considerable influence on the headteacher's allocation of scholarships and bursaries.

As all the good private schools are selective they each have their own 11+ (be aware they tend to call it a **common entrance exam**) you therefore need to approach each one separately to find out the details. And, some exams are harder than others. The harder ones are set by the higher achieving schools because they are looking to recruit only the most academic pupils. What this means in reality is that some private schools are harder to get into than others and are therefore more prestigious. If you think about it, though, that's no different to the state system.

Interestingly, private school 11+'s tend to differ to the state school exams. For a start, they are not obsessed with verbal and non verbal reasoning and none that I know set both papers (though many set one) The subject they all favour that, for some reason the state schools don't, is English. An essay and a English comprehension test play a part in most of the independent school exams. So, if your child has a creative bent, an analytical mind and the ability to string words together effectively and accurately, then they're already half way there, whereas in the state sector these qualities at 11+ are of little value.

Independent schools hold their exams in January and for most of them you need to register by the end of November. At this stage almost all of them require a non-returnable registration fee of around £60. If you ask them what it's for they'll say it's to cover admin costs, but you don't need to be Pythagoras to work out that what it's really for is to boost their coffers. Think about it, if 350 children take an exam (often it's more) and each pay £60, that's a whopping £21,000. Nice work if you can get it!

Just like the state sector all the independent schools hold open events where you can look round, talk to teachers, pupils etc. And they all produce the same documents for you to peruse – prospectuses, brochures etc. Some provide specimen questions to help you prepare for the exam, others don't. Some tell you the specific syllabus subjects that could be tested in maths, while others just refer you to topics on the National Curriculum.

Because they're independent and govern themselves, private schools can do pretty much what they like - as long as it's within the law. What this means is that no two are the same. The trick to deciding which one might suit your child is by getting to know them and understanding their different ethoses, principles and attitudes to work, discipline, and respect. Look at their social, cultural and racial mixes, look at their achievement levels and exam results, look at the subjects they study and look at the parents. Are they *your sort* of people? Do you *want* them to be your sort of people or do you want something different for your son and daughter? If the school's snobby and posh and you're not, is that a good or a bad thing for your child? And if *you* are snobby and posh, is it important that your child only mixes with similar people or do you want them to live in a more down-to-earth world?

So, while all the conventional dilemmas about choosing the right school exist in the same way as they do in the state system, there are other moral and ethical issues at stake which, in some ways, make the decision more difficult.

Maybe you'll decide a private school is not for you. I know pushy middle-class parents who could easily afford the fees but chose to send their child to a state grammar. I know affluent people with left wing politics who decided their bright child should not go to a private or grammar school but the local comprehensive rated 'satisfactory' by Ofsted. I know an out-of-work single mother with pushy parent tendencies who 'played' the independent school system and came out with a place at one of the most prestigious private girls' schools in London – with 100% funding!

The arguments for and against independent schooling VS the state system are numerous. The issue is one of the biggest education conundrums of our time. Many people believe the UK education system is unfair because the state/private divide creates an educational apartheid with your ability to pay determining which side of the line you fall.

I will not expand, as this book is not about the subject. There are, however, certain *indisputable facts* which if you are weighing up the pros and cons of private VS state maybe of use to you:

- Private schools have smaller class sizes, better facilities and they dominate academic league tables and entry to top universities. They are also very expensive.
- State schools are the 'norm' (only 7.5% of all children are in private education), they are free and they are non-elitist.

I suggest that whatever conclusions you come to, they should be based on how you hope your child will turn out and whether you think the school will enable them to achieve what they're truly capable of.

After all, fulfilling their potential is the most we can hope for our children, isn't it?

# A FINAL WORD...

## <u>WHAT IT'S LIKE FOR A CHILD</u>

**By Sienna Jane Fox White, age, 11, who went through the 11+ process and survived.**

**She says:**

"The 11+ is a make-or-break exam that will change your life. If you pass it you'll go to a good school, if you fail it, you probably won't.  If you are a child with a pushy parent you will understand this from a young age and you're not allowed to forget it until the exam's over.

I know it's important to work hard so that you can pass the exams and I spent about 18 months doing extra stuff after school so that I was ready for them. But it really gets in the way of the things you want to do and it was a bit stressful and not much fun.

My mum and I got into rows because I often didn't want to do the work. She would also get grumpy with me if I kept getting the same things wrong or I forgot how to do something. Her favourite thing to get annoyed about was when I didn't check my work when I'd finished it, or when I rushed work and made careless mistakes.

I admit I did do those things quite a lot, but that was just because I wanted to get the work over and done with.

I think if your parent is going to act as your teacher then it's important they are patient. I know this must be hard sometimes because children are good at winding-up adults. My mum always used to be saying to me things like, "you wouldn't say that to your teacher would you?" and I knew she was right, but there's something very different about a parent trying to teach you - somehow you can't take them as seriously.

The best way to start the extra work is slowly. My mum tried to make some of it fun and it did help. She also had a reward system where if I did the work for a week without a big fuss, she would get me a little gift like a book or a cuddly toy. This at least made it a bit worthwhile although there were many weeks when I got nothing!

Things changed when I got a tutor and I realised I had to knuckle down. I think I worked pretty hard most of the time and as my marks in practice papers got better by the week it was very rewarding.

At school we talked about 11+ a lot. Most of my friends were in the same boat as me with all the extra work and we would swap stories of what was going on at home, not all of it was nice! We all felt under pressure to do well. That came partly from our parents but partly because at the school I went to almost everyone takes the 11+ and it's normal to get stressed about it. At least we had each other for support. It would have been awful going through it alone.

Our parents were more stressed about it than us which I thought was quite funny! When they met in the street the 11+ and secondary schools was all they talked about. I wondered why they didn't get bored, I also wondered why *they* were stressed when it was us – not them - who had to do the exams.

As the exams got nearer I got more and more nervous. Luckily I was able to do a practice test which was exactly like the real one a week later. That really helped because I knew what to expect and was familiar with the organisation of it all.

All in all, I did 14 different papers and I was relieved when they were all over. Exams are not nice, but even as a child you accept they are part of your life because they're a means to an end. In my case, the exams I found hard I passed easily and vice versa. I have never understood why this was.

Waiting for the results feels like a lifetime. Hopefully your child will pass, but if they don't there are things that can be done; it doesn't necessarily mean they won't be able to go to a good school.

And if they do pass, they will feel a massive sense of achievement that stays with them for a long time. It's at this point they will realise that all their hard work was worth it and hopefully they will appreciate yours too.

Finally, if you are lucky enough to be able to choose your child's school, make sure they're happy with it too. I think the child should help make the decision because they're the ones who will be spending the next seven years of their life there, not you.

I wish you every success for the metaphoric car journey that is the 11+. Expect punctures, flat batteries, engine trouble and breakdowns along the way but when you arrive at your destination the relief will be enormous!"

# Appendix

## TIMETABLE OF KEY DATES

| WHEN | WHAT HAPPENS |
| --- | --- |
| **May-mid July** | Register for Bexley tests |
| **June – 1st July** | Register for Kent tests |
| **End of June (30th in 2012)** | Olave's open day |
| **Early July (6th in 2012)** | Olave's/Newstead's supplementary form in |
| **Mid July onwards** | Obtain education authority brochures |
| **September 1st** | School application period starts |
| **Early September** | 11+ test centre allocations/times sent out |
| **Mid–late September** | 11+ Exams |
| **September – October** | School open events |
| **Around October 12th** | Bexley and Newstead results |
| **Around October 17th** | Kent results |
| **Before half-term** | CAF form recommended to be in by |

| | |
|---|---|
| **October 31<sup>st</sup>** | CAF form *must* be in by |
| **End of November** school entrance exams | Register for private |
| **Mid December** | Bexley 11+ re-take |
| **Christmas** results | Bexley 11+ re-take |
| **January** exams | Private school entrance |
| **Mid February** results/offers sent out | Private school |
| **March 1st** out | State school offers sent |
| ***Around March 5th*** school offers | Accept/decline private |
| **March 15<sup>th</sup>/16<sup>th</sup>** school offers | Accept/decline state |
| **March 15<sup>th</sup>/16<sup>th</sup>** lodging Appeals | Closing date for |
| **May/June** | Appeal hearings |
| **April-September** established | Waiting lists |

# FURTHER INFORMATION

## 11+Websites providing information, practice resources and online tutoring:

- www.elevenplusadvice.co.uk
- www.elevenplus.net
- www.elevenplusexams.co.uk
- www.11plus.co.uk
- www.the11pluswebsite.co.uk
- www.11plusknowledge.co.uk
- www.11plusswot.co.uk
- www.elevenplus.com
- www.11pl.us
- www.tutr.co.uk
- www.bofa11plus.com
- www.bond11plus.co.uk

## Useful school and educational websites:

- www.bbc.co.uk/schools
- www.bbc.co.uk/education
- www.bbc.co.uk/learning
- www.bbc.co.uk/schools/parents
- www.education.org
- www.topmarks.co.uk

- www.goodschoolsguide.co.uk
- www.schoolswebdirectory.co.uk
- www.schoolsnet.com
- www.tigerchild.com

## Independent Sector:

- www.isc.co.uk
- www.indschools.co.uk
- www.schoolsearch.co.uk

## Government and Education:

- www.education.gov.uk (Department of Education)
- www.dfes.gov.uk/performancetables (school league tables)
- www.ofsted.gov.uk (school inspection reports)